THE GREAT SWINDLE

The Great Swindle

THE STORY OF THE

SOUTH SEA BUBBLE

BY

Virginia Cowles

COLLINS

ST JAMES'S PLACE, LONDON

1960

© Crawley Features, 1960
Printed in Great Britain
Collins Clear-Type Press
London and Glasgow

CONTENTS

ILLUSTRATIONS

7

THE EARL OF OXFORD

WHEN the South Sea Company was formed in the year 1711, it was hailed by partisans as " the Earl of Oxford's masterpiece." From the beginning it was no ordinary company. The Earl, better known as Mr. Robert Harley, called it into being as an adroit move in one of the most ruthless political battles in history. So let us open our story in 1709, with Mr. Harley, sword drawn, waiting to strike.

Queen Anne's ministers were not having an easy time. In the autumn, Her Majesty's Treasurer, Lord Godolphin, called on the directors of the Bank of England and asked for a loan of £600,000 to carry on the war against France. His request was granted; but before he left, the Governor of the Bank, Sir Gilbert Heathcote, said:

" Pray, my Lord, don't let us have a rotten peace."

" Pray, tell me, what do you call a rotten peace? "

" I call anything a rotten peace unless we have Spain, for without it we can have no safety, and now we have them down, let us keep them so, till we get quite out of the war."

" But, Sir Gilbert, I want you a little to consider the circumstances of the Duke of Marlborough and me; we are railed at every day for having a mind, as they call it, to perpetuate the war, and we are told we shall be worried next winter, for refusing a good peace, and insisting upon terms which it is impossible for France to perform."

" They are a company of rotten rogues that tell you so," replied Sir Gilbert. " I'll warrant you, we'll stand by you."

England had been at war for twenty years with only one,

uneasy interlude of peace from 1697 to 1701. The superficial
reasons for the war changed, but the fundamental cause was
constant: to prevent Louis XIV from dominating the continent
of Europe. The Whig party believed passionately that if any
single power established a hegemony, England's freedom would
be in peril; her trade routes would be threatened and her prosperity endangered. The Tories took a different view. They
were the aristocrats and squires—" the gentlemen of England "
they called themselves. They hated the war because the
land-owners bore the brunt of the taxes while the Whig
merchants prospered by lending out their money at high rates
of interest. They wanted to lead their country lives in peace,
and regarded foreign affairs as a nuisance. They were, in fact,
isolationists.

Their voices were scarcely audible during the first years of
the Queen's reign. Anne was directed by a powerful triumvirate
composed of the Duke and Duchess of Marlborough and Lord
Godolphin. These three carried out the Whig war policy with
rigid determination and remarkable efficiency. " Sarah managed
the Queen, Marlborough managed the war and Godolphin
managed the Parliament." In order to make his task easier,
however, Godolphin invited Mr. Robert Harley to join the
Cabinet in 1702. Harley was a Tory but he had won a reputation
as a moderate. He had a thorough knowledge of the House of
Commons; he had spent years building up a network of contacts
and making a study of the party machinery. He was a strangely
unattractive figure. A dark, heavy man with sensual lips, he
spoke with " serpentine convulsions " and found it difficult to
express himself. Even when he managed to get the words out,
it was not easy to understand what he meant. " That lord,"
wrote Pope, " talked of business in so confused a manner that
you did not know what he was all about; and everything was
in the epic way for he always began in the middle." This may
have been due to drink, although as Macaulay pointed out,
" his practice of flustering himself daily with claret was hardly

considered a fault by his contemporaries." Harley's character, like his language was difficult to plumb. Macaulay contended that his dullness and diffuseness were his greatest assets. " It is soothing to believe that what is splendid cannot be solid, that what is clear cannot be profound . . . From the absence of show in Harley's discourses many people inferred that there must be much substance; and he was pronounced to be a deep-read, deep-thinking gentleman, not a fine talker, but fitter to direct affairs of State than all the fine talkers in the world. This character he long supported with that cunning which is frequently found in company with ambitious and unquiet mediocrity. He constantly had, even with his best friends, an air of mystery and reserve which seemed to indicate that he knew some momentous secret, and that his mind was labouring with some vast design . . ."[1] Harley's design was neither vast nor noble, nevertheless it was real. Through the muddy waters flashed a diamond-hard determination to advance himself at any cost. His " sources" of information covered the whole country; he paid people to report to him; he understood every nuance of the party game. He was an expert operator.

For some time, he served Godolphin and the Marlboroughs faithfully. There was little else he could do. Marlborough, in conjunction with Prince Eugene of Savoy, led England and the Grand Alliance to a succession of victories. Blenheim and Ramillies covered Queen Anne's reign with glory and lifted the nation to a pinnacle of fame. The Queen could not do enough for her beloved " Mr. and Mrs. Freeman "—the intimate names she had given to the Marlboroughs. Once when Sarah wrote a foolish letter about the Duke and herself resigning their offices, the Queen replied pathetically, " If ever you should forsake me, I would have nothing more to do with the world, but make another abdication; for what is a crown when the support of it is gone. I will never forsake your dear self, Mr. Freeman, nor Mr. Montgomery [Lord Godolphin] but always be your constant

[1] *History of England*: Lord Macaulay.

faithful servant; and we four must never part, till death mows us down with his impartial hand.''[1]

There was no doubt that Sarah was the lynch-pin of the triumvirate. She had exercised a strange fascination for the Queen ever since childhood. '' We used to play together when she was a child, and she even then expressed a fondness for me,'' wrote Sarah. When the Queen ascended the throne Sarah was forty-one and her domination was as strong as ever. Anne heaped her with honours. She made her Mistress of the Robes, Groom of the Stole and Comptroller of the Privy Purse. Apart from the Queen, Sarah was the most powerful woman in the land. She saw that the wishes of Marlborough and Godolphin were executed. She was courted by statesmen and ambassadors. She had the standing of a Cabinet minister.

It was not easy to carry on her work, run her houses, and at the same time be at the Queen's beck and call. Anne was exacting. She would have been pleased to have '' Mrs. Freeman '' constantly at her side. Sarah was at her wits' end how to provide the Queen with the hours of companionship she desired. Suddenly she hit upon an idea. Perhaps Abigail Hill would divert her. Abigail played the harpsichord enchantingly, an instrument which the Queen particularly liked. If Anne could be persuaded to take the girl as a Dresser, it might offer a solution.

Abigail Hill was a poor relation. Sarah's grandfather, Sir John Jennings, had produced twenty-two children. One of them, a sister of Sarah's father, had married a Levantine merchant by the name of Hill. This man had lost his money speculating; and when he and his wife died, their four children were penniless. Oddly enough, Sarah had never heard of them. One day she received a letter, explaining who they were and telling of their plight. She stepped into the breach and found them jobs. She invited the eldest girl, Abigail, to live with her at St. Albans as one of the family. Abigail was in her early twenties. She was attractive, good-tempered and efficient. Besides her talents with

[1] *Marlborough—His Life and Times*: Winston S. Churchill.

the harpsichord, she had the patience to make a good nurse. The Queen had borne seventeen children, none of whom survived. Her body was racked by physical strain, and now she suffered from gout as well. She could use a willing and able attendant.

Anne accepted Abigail as her Dresser but for some time her demands on Sarah did not lessen. Indeed, once when Sarah did Abigail a kindness by inviting her to the opera, the Queen wrote her a strange, jealous letter. " Dear Mrs. Freeman hates writing so much I fear, though she would stay away two or three days, she would hardly let me hear from her, and therefore for my own sake I must write to get a line or two. I fancy now you are in town you will be tempted to see the opera, which I should not wonder at, for I should be so too, if I were able to stir, but when that will be God knows, for my feavor is not quite gone, and I am still so lame I cannot go without limping. I hope Mrs. Freeman has no thoughts of going to the opera with Mistress Hill, and will have a care of engaging herself too much in her company, for, if you give way to that, it is a thing that will insensibly grow upon you. Therefore give me leave once more to beg for your own sake, as well as poor Mrs. Morley's, that you would have as little to do with that enchantress as 'tis possible, and pray pardon me for saying this."[1]

It is difficult to put a finger on the moment when the rift between the Queen and Sarah began. Temperamentally, the two women were very different. Sarah was a Whig and a rebel and no respecter of established order. The Queen, on the other hand, was deeply conservative. She hated the Whig Party. The fact that the Whigs were espousing her cause, by fighting Louis XIV who would put her Stuart half-brother on the English throne if he could, made her hate them all the more. She believed in the Divine Right of Kings. She squared her conscience by insisting that the Pretender was not really her brother at all. Sarah's

[1] *Marlborough—His Life and Times*: Winston S. Churchill.

Whiggery annoyed her. The Duchess had no respect for the Established Church and upheld the right of Parliament to select the Princes that served its purpose. Before Anne had become Queen, she had avoided talking politics with Sarah; but now it was inescapable. Quite apart from political differences, Sarah was tactless. She was hot-tempered and impulsive and spoke much too bluntly. " I was convinced that Princes were ruined by flatterers," she wrote. " I carried this so far, as to think it was a part of flattery, not to tell her everything that was in any sort amisse in her."

The two women began to quarrel. The first quarrel was over Marlborough's son-in-law, the Earl of Sunderland. The Whig Party insisted that Sunderland be included in the Government and the Queen refused to have him. She suspected him of republicanism and loathed him. Godolphin pressed Sarah to make her change her mind; without Sunderland the Whig Party would obstruct supplies for the war. Sarah opened a correspondence with the Queen which stretched over the months. First it was acrimonious, then angry. In the end Anne was obliged to give in, but she did not conceal her resentment. Once emotions had died down, Sarah expected her to warm again. They had quarrelled before and, in time, Anne always melted. But on this occasion the Queen remained aloof and hostile. With a shock, Sarah sensed that her feelings had undergone a permanent change. She was alarmed and puzzled.

She could not understand it until she heard that Abigail Hill had married one of the Prince's gentlemen, a Mr. Masham. The fact that the girl, whom she had looked after like a daughter, had not bothered to tell her, revealed everything. Abigail was working against her. Sarah was not one to hide her emotions. She stormed to the palace and confronted Mrs. Masham. " I began to tell her that it was very plain the Queen was much changed towards me, and that I could not attribute this to anything but her secret management; that I knew she had been very frequently with her Majesty in private, and that the very attempt to conceal this, by artifice, from such a friend as I had been to her was alone a very ill sign, and enough to prove a very bad purpose at bottom. To this she very gravely answered that *she was sure the Queen who had loved me extremely, would always be very kind to me.* It was some minutes before I could recover from the surprise with which so extraordinary an answer struck me. To see a woman, whom I had raised out of the dust, put on such a superior air, and to hear her assure me, by way of consolation, that the Queen would be always very kind to me! At length I went on to reproach her with her ingratitude and her secret management with the Queen to undermine those who had so long and with so much honour served her Majesty."[1]

It was a queer stroke of fate that had brought Abigail Hill into the world as a relation both of the Duchess of Marlborough and Mr. Robert Harley. Like Sarah, Harley had no idea of Abigail's existence until he received a letter pointing out her connection with his mother's family. He paid scant attention to her, however, until she became the Queen's Dresser. Then one day the gardener delivered him a note, in which Abigail asked his help in advising the Queen. It was irresistible. From that moment Harley began to plot. He kept his meetings with Abigail secret. He told her to widen the rift between Sarah and the Queen, and supplied useful bits of poison. Abigail was an apt pupil. She smoothed the Queen's pillows, played the harpsichord, and repeated injurious gossip with an air of innocence. She frequently arranged meetings between Harley and the Queen. These, too, were conducted " up the back stairs."

Abigail was not a clever woman, and Sarah realised that someone must be guiding her. Harley's intrigue was carried on so privately that it was some time before she discovered his role. When she became aware of it, she sensed real danger. She had always disliked and distrusted him. Now it was apparent that

[1] *Conduct*: Sarah, Duchess of Marlborough.

he was playing for the highest stakes. He would try to overthrow Godolphin and install himself as Treasurer. He almost succeeded. Jonathan Swift wrote to Stella, " Mr. Harley had been some time, with the greatest art imaginable, carrying on an intrigue to alter the Ministry, and began with no less an enterprise than that of removing the Lord Chancellor, and had nearly effected it by the help of Mrs. Masham, one of the Queen's Dressers, who was a great and growing favourite, of much industry and insinuation . . . [He] had laid a scheme for an entire new Ministry, and the men are named to whom the several employments were to be given; and though his project has miscarried, it is reckoned the greatest piece of Court skill that has been acted these many years."[1]

How had Harley's plans miscarried? The Duke of Marlborough had taken immediate action. He had called on the Queen and told her bluntly that unless she dismissed Harley without delay he himself would resign. The Queen knew she could not afford to lose the services of the most illustrious man in Europe, much less try and conduct the war without him. She wept and stormed and seemed nearly to suffocate. She told him " he might as well draw his dagger and stab her then and there as do such a thing." Yet, with true Stuart obstinacy she refused to agree. A week later Marlborough wrote her a final letter. " Madame, Since all the faithful services I have endeavoured to do you, and the unwearied pains I have taken for these ten days to satisfy and convince your Majesty's own mind, have not been able to give you any such impressions of the false and treacherous proceedings of Mr. Secretary Harley to Lord Treasurer and myself, but that your Majesty is pleased to countenance and support him, to the ruin of your own business at home, I am very much afraid it will be attended with the sorrow and amazement of all Europe, as soon as the noise of it gets abroad. And I find myself obliged . . . to acquaint your Majesty that no consideration can make me serve any longer with that man. And I beseech

[1] *Prose Works*: Jonathan Swift.

Robert Harley, 1st Earl of Oxford, founder and first Governor of the South Sea Company

your Majesty to look upon me, from this moment, as forced out of your service as long as you think fit to continue him in it."[1]

Anne still refused to give in. Incredible as it seems, with the war approaching a climax, she accepted Marlborough's resignation along with Godolphin's. The situation, of course, was grotesque. When the Cabinet Council met, Harley rose to open the business. The Duke of Somerset also rose and interrupted Harley: "If your Majesty suffers that fellow to treat of affairs of the war without the General, I cannot serve you."[2] Harley faltered and the Duke repeated what he had said. The ministers gathered their papers in embarrassed silence and the Council broke up in confusion. Harley saw that he was beaten. There was nothing for him to do but hand his resignation to the Queen. She wept and he departed.

Harley's downfall was only temporary. In 1708 England and her allies muffed the chance to make peace. Louis XIV would have accepted almost any terms to stop the war; his armies had been so severely mauled, never again would they take the offensive. The Dutch were weary, the English divided. The right moment had come for an armistice. But the conditions demanded by the Whig Party were impossible for the French King to fulfil. The war had started because Louis had placed his grandson, Philip V on the throne of Spain. England would not tolerate what almost amounted to a federation between the two strongest powers on the Continent. Philip must go. Louis XIV pointed out that he had no power to evict him. Philip refused to budge. In that case, replied the Whigs, Louis must join the Allies and remove him by force. This was an impossible condition. The French Foreign Minister was shocked when he heard it. When he reported it to Louis, the King remarked wearily that it was more than flesh and blood could stand. "If

---

[1] *Memoirs of the Duke of Marlborough*: W. C. Coxe
[2] *Prose Works*: Jonathan Swift.

I must fight," he flashed, "it shall be with my enemies, rather than my children." And the war continued.

Harley became leader of the Tory Peace Party. There was nothing discreditable in working for peace; but the methods he employed produced a series of the most disgraceful episodes in British history. He revelled in duplicity—which some malicious persons put down to his Welsh ancestry. He employed a band of intellectuals, the "angry young men" of the day, to travel about England and report the state of public opinion to him. Even this operation was shrouded in mystery; he liked people to refer to his private "intelligence service." One of his correspondents was Daniel Defoe, who was to become celebrated as the author of *Robinson Crusoe*; another was the poet and diplomatist Matthew Prior; another, a Cambridge graduate and school-master by the name of Erasmus Lewis. Lewis was full of spleen and supplied Harley with the sort of gossip he liked. The value of his reports is difficult to determine, for his appraisal of Marl-borough's ability as a general does not give one much confidence. "You would be surprised to hear men say publicly," he wrote to Harley, "we have spent so many millions to find out this great secret, that our General does not understand the *métier de la guerre*, that he had indeed twice or thrice thrown a lucky main, but never knew how to play his game, and that he is but a little genius . . ."[1]

Harley's young men informed him of the growing pressure for peace throughout the length and breadth of England. But it took the famous Sacheverell trial to make it apparent to all. Sacheverell was a Tory parson, who delivered a sermon at St. Paul's attacking the Government, the Whigs and Lord Godolphin. He preached conservatism in its highest form; the Divine Right of Kings, the sanctity of the Established Church, and above all, peace. He described Godolphin as a "wily Volpone." For some time Godolphin had complained of "the insolences of the clergy." He did not want them meddling in the mounting political

[1] *Portland Papers.*

crisis. Someone suggested impeaching Sacheverell as a traitor, on the grounds that his utterances on Divine Right were designed to undermine the Act of Parliament and the Hanoverian Succession.

The trial took place in Westminster Hall. Sir Christopher Wren erected the scaffolding; Sacheverell drove every day to the scene in a glass coach; and society scrambled for tickets. Lady Wentworth declared that the trial would make " all the Ladys turn good huswivs, they goe att seven every morning " to secure seats. And a leading actor complained that " our audiences were extremely weakened during the trial, by the better rank of people's daily attending it." There was no doubt, judging by the tumultuous crowds that swarmed round Sacheverell's coach, that public opinion was on the side of the clergyman. The House of Lords found him guilty by only seventeen votes, which was almost as good as an acquittal. Consequently his sentence was ridiculously light; simply to refrain from preaching for three years.

Sacheverell had accomplished far more than he planned when he wrote his sermon. By revealing widespread support for the Tory Peace Party, he gave Harley the victory he longed for. The Queen plucked up courage to adopt the policy he had been urging upon her. First, she sacked Marlborough's son-in-law, Lord Sunderland. Then, a few months later she sent a curt message dismissing her counsellor of thirty years, Lord Godolphin, and offering him a pension of £4,000 a year. Godolphin broke the White Staff and declined the pension. Only Marlborough remained. The war was still going on and the Government could not do without him. Although he was stripped of all political power he was bidden, as a soldier, to remain at his post. Harley became Chancellor of the Exchequer in Godolphin's place, and virtual head of the Government.

A few weeks later the Queen dissolved Parliament and one of the rowdiest general elections ever known took place. Each side accused the other of getting the voters drunk to secure their support. However, one honest miller declared, " I am always drunk for a week at every election and I won't vote for the man who won't make me drunk." The Tories swept the country, and the Whigs were beaten by more than two to one. At last Harley had the support of the Commons as well as the Queen. He brought into office with him the brilliant, dissipated Henry St. John, who later became Lord Bolingbroke. Along with Abigail these three made up the new triumvirate. The Duke of Buckinghamshire did not think much of the trio, and was said to have exclaimed " Good God, how has this poor nation been governed in my time! During the reign of King Charles the Second we were governed by a parcel of French whores, in King James the Second's time by a parcel of Popish priests, in King William's time by a parcel of Dutch footmen, and now we are governed by a dirty chambermaid, a Welch attorney, and a profligate wretch that has neither honour or honesty."

Harley's first aim was to draw up a draft peace treaty. Although England had solemnly promised her Allies—the Dutch, the Austrians, the various German states—that she would neither seek nor negotiate a secret peace treaty, Harley was not the sort of man to consider himself bound by a pledge. It would have been incompatible with his nature to inform the members of the alliance that England was ready to recognise Louis XIV's grandson as King of Spain—the refusal of which had sparked off the war—and try to work out a peace plan with them. Instead, he decided to send the Earl of Jersey to Paris to carry on clandestine conversations with Louis' ministers, in flagrant breach of the assurances that had been made. No one knew about the talks; not the Cabinet, not the Parliament, not even the Duke of Marlborough, who was still leading the army.

While these talks were taking place, Harley turned his attention to internal affairs. The national debt was enormous, and the Bank of England was not being helpful. It had no constructive suggestions to make, and Harley sensed an atmosphere of cold hostility. This feeling was mutual. If there was any single institution Harley hated it was the Bank. His enmity stemmed back many years to the time he had tried to set up a rival institution and had been made to look ridiculous. It had happened a few years after he entered Parliament. William and Mary were on the throne and William was desperate for money to carry on the war against France. Mr. Charles Montagu, afterwards Lord Halifax, outlined a solution to Parliament in 1694, based on the proposal of a Scot, Mr. William Paterson. A bank would be founded. Its stock would be sold to private subscribers for £1,200,000, and the money lent to the Government at 8% interest.

The idea of a bank appalled the Tory landowners. They called attention to the most famous banks on the Continent—those of Amsterdam and Genoa—and pointed out that such institutions only flourished in republics. Furthermore, they declared, a bank financed by Whig merchants—as this one would be—might dominate the political life of the country and ruin the landed interests. The Whigs countered by insisting that the goldsmiths were not proving satisfactory bankers, for not a single one of them could supply sufficient money for the war. The goldsmiths had drifted into banking by accident. Their chief business was embossing pistol handles and fashioning silver buckles. But since they possessed large vaults, immune from fire and theft, individuals and even private firms had begun to deposit valuables with them. This habit became so widespread that when the well-known financier, Sir Dudley North, returned to London in 1680, after twenty years in the Levant, he was amazed to find himself followed along the streets of the City by goldsmiths begging to serve him. Repeatedly he was asked where he kept his money, and each time he replied testily: " Where should I keep it but in my own house? "

North could not be persuaded to participate in the new banking system and in some respects he was right. Although on the whole the goldsmiths won a reputation for reliability and their notes circulated freely among business firms, many of them went bankrupt. They made profits on the money in their care (for which they often paid no interest since they were doing the owners a service) by lending it out at astronomical rates of interest, sometimes as high as 33%. They grew rich rapidly when their clients paid up, but when a black sheep or two scampered off, bankruptcy was apt to follow. An eminent financier of the day, Michael Godfrey, declared that two or three million pounds were lost in ten years by goldsmiths " breaking."

Despite the heated Tory opposition, Mr. Charles Montagu's contention that a bank had become a dire necessity, won the day; and in 1694 the Bank of England—a purely private company despite its grandiose name—came into being. The proposed sum of £1,200,000 was raised within a few hours, the Duke and Duchess of Marlborough subscribing £10,000 and Lord Godolphin £7,000. The new Company was a revolutionary institution. Whereas its continental rivals existed merely as places of safe-keeping, or as government creditors, the Bank of England took the unprecedented step of issuing notes " payable to bearer "— bank notes as we know them to-day. Up until now, the only notes circulating in England were goldsmiths' pledges made out to specific persons—like modern cheques. " Payable to bearer," meant that the new notes could move freely from hand to hand. Since the Bank had raised £1,200,000 for the Government it was allowed to issue the same amount in paper notes.

The Company did well from the start, but two years later, in 1696, the King again was in need of money, and the infant bank was not strong enough to make a second loan. Young Mr. Harley had been searching for a cause which would ingratiate him with the Tory Party, and hit upon the idea of a " Land Bank." This company would raise not one million, but two million pounds—and no Whig merchant would be allowed to subscribe. It would lend most of its money to the Government at 7% interest, the rest would be put aside so that needy Tory squires could borrow at low rates of interest to repair their barns and roofs.

The Tories were delighted with the picture, and overnight Harley became the toast of the Party. The Whig members of Parliament, on an appeal of patriotism, were induced to give the project their support and an act of authorisation was passed. A meeting to explain the plan was held in the Hall of the Middle Temple, and forty agents were sent into the shires to acquaint the landed gentry with the details. Two offices were opened to receive the subscriptions. The first five thousand pounds was put down in the King's name, and the clerks waited at their desks, books open, for the money to pour in. But no money came. At the end of three weeks only fifteen hundred pounds had been subscribed. It then became clear that the enthusiasm of the landed gentry for the bank had been based on the fact that they wished to borrow money at low rates; and " wishing to borrow money they were not in a position to lend it." Indeed, the only people who could lend it were the merchants who were forbidden to subscribe. So the scheme fell to the ground. Nevertheless, it had managed to do great harm. It had nearly wrecked the infant Bank of England by frightening people from making deposits; they felt there would not be room for two institutions of the same kind. Bank stock fell sharply.

King William was left on a limb, for Harley had promised him over a million pounds. He was in Flanders with the army and instructed his agent, the Duke of Shrewsbury, to go to the Bank of England and tell the directors that if he did not receive a minimum of £200,000 cash, his soldiers would desert. Knowing the Bank's difficulties, Shrewsbury undertook his task gloomily. " If this should not succeed," he said, " God knows what can be done. Anything must be tried and ventured rather than lie down and die." The Bank directors held a General Court and appealed to their shareholders to advance another 20% to the Government. Moved by patriotism, the vote was unanimous. William was saved, and the war went on.

Now, fifteen years later, Harley was Chancellor of the Exchequer,[1] and the Bank was the pride of the nation. Its prestige only served to increase his rancour. One of his first acts, as Chancellor, was to try and organise an eighteenth-century takeover bid. Every year the Bank held a shareholders' meeting to elect its directors. The plan was that the Tory shareholders would attend *en bloc*, catch the Whigs napping, and vote their own men into office. The plot misfired. Somehow Sarah Marlborough got wind of it and organised a rapid defence. She wrote letters to her Whig friends and acquaintances abjuring them to turn up at the meeting; and had some sharp words for those too lazy to make the journey from the country. Lord Hervey was one of them. In vain his wife wrote to him: " Thursday is the day of the election, and the Duchess of Marlborough says it is a terrible reflection upon anybody that can stay to see a horse race though there were but a possibility of the Bank of England put into ill hands by it; and, if the Tories get the better, Mr. Hopkins says you all may make use of your horses to run away."[2] However, in the midst of high excitement, the Whigs carried their candidates, and the Company remained in the hands of its originators.

If Harley could not capture the Bank, he must set up a rival organisation. He discussed the matter with one of his young men—Daniel Defoe, who had always been interested in economics. Defoe was a pathetic character, who was almost entirely dependent on Harley for his living. For years he had been writing pamphlets on trade and suggesting " projects " from which the Government could reap new wealth. Not that he, himself, had been very successful as a money-maker. His whole life had been spent trying to escape the clutches of his creditors. His father was a candle-merchant and when Defoe left school he was apprenticed to a haberdashery firm. He had

---

[1] The office of First Lord of the Treasury was put into commission when Godolphin was dismissed.

[2] *Letter-Books of John Hervey.*

done a certain amount of travelling in order to learn the ways of commerce (his enemies jeered at him as a hosiery salesman) and when he finished his apprenticeship, decided to seek his fortune as a merchant. He had dabbled in all sorts of ventures; had taken shares in trading vessels; had set up a brick factory; had bought a farm of civet-cats, valuable for making scent. His ideas of honesty were rather peculiar for he sold his civet-cats several times over and defrauded his mother-in-law of £400. More than once he was sued in the courts, and in 1692 he went bankrupt for £17,000. He fled to Bristol and went into hiding to escape the debtors' prison. In those days debtors were free from arrest on the Sabbath, and Defoe became known as " the Sunday gentleman." He came out of hiding on this day only and paraded through the town in a fashionable, curly wig and flowing lace cuffs. However, during the next thirteen years, by various forms of promotion and speculation, he apparently paid off twelve thousand pounds of debts. Ironically enough, it was his political writing, not his business miscalculations, which finally landed him in gaol. One of his essays was regarded as an attack on the Church of England and he was sentenced to three days in the pillory and an indefinite term in Newgate Prison. At this point Robert Harley had come to his rescue. He recognised Defoe's talents as a pamphleteer and decided to use him as a propagandist.

Defoe started his news-sheet *The Review* and served Harley faithfully for many years. He was never free from financial worry for it was part of Harley's policy to keep him short of money and make him continuously aware of his dependence. There are many letters from him pressing his benefactor to send remuneration. " I am forced by importuning circumstances to remind you that of the allowances of appointment, which by your intercession or Her Majesty's goodness I enjoy, these are two quarters behind . . ."[1]

Now Defoe set himself to work afresh on Harley's problems.

[1] *Harley Papers.*

They were very varied; not only did the Chancellor seek to lessen the influence of the Bank of England, but to cut down the high rate of interest the Government was paying on its loans; and thirdly, to secure the peace. A few weeks later Harley had a plan, believed to be Defoe's, which solved all three. It was a work of genius. It was the South Sea scheme.

Defoe had always been fascinated by South America. Indeed, when he created Robinson Crusoe nine years later he cast his hero upon an island off the South American coast. The idea of a company to trade with this part of the world had been fermenting in his mind for many years. He even may have outlined it to William of Orange. His thesis was that there was a fortune to be made from this continent if only the labour could be produced to develop the country. Why not import slaves from Africa on a really large scale? If new colonies could be planted fresh gold quarries might be discovered, and the more people who settled there, the more outlet for English goods, wool in particular.

The brilliance of this project, from Harley's point of view, was that it dovetailed perfectly with his political aims, and at the same time solved his pressing problems. In addition to the money the Government had borrowed from the Bank of England, it owed nearly £10,000,000 to private lenders. If Harley could persuade these creditors to accept shares in the South Sea Company as payment, the Government would be relieved of an enormous burden. It would only have to find the money to pay the interest. And if the South Sea Company prospered, why should it not rival the Bank of England and give the Whigs a run for their money? It might furnish the " gentlemen of England " with the financial power they had always coveted. For perhaps most important of all, was the consideration that if Parliament incorporated the South Sea Company whose aim was to trade with the King of Spain's subjects in South America, it would have to support Harley in seeking peace. Government finance would be inextricably bound to a cessation of hostilities.

Politically, Defoe's scheme was a masterpiece. It gave Harley everything he wanted. Morally, it left much to be desired. In the first place, England had solemnly promised the Dutch to share with them any trade concessions to South America; and, of course, there was the tiresome pledge not to sign a separate peace at all. Financially, the scheme had disadvantages as well. It was all very well for England to grant the Company a monopoly to South America, but England's jurisdiction did not extend beyond her own shores. What about the Spanish? Would they agree to let the English have exclusive trading rights with their South American colonies? The French were the present tenants of the monopoly, but they had derived little benefit from it due to the interference of the English Navy. Would Louis relinquish the privilege?

In the spring of 1711 the peace talks had been going on for nine months. They were progressing so slowly that Harley decided to send one of his young men, Matthew Prior, to Paris to get something committed to paper. Although Prior was an experienced diplomatist as well as a poet, the Queen was not sure that he was the right person to go. " I have always thought it wrong," she said, " to send people abroad of meane extraction; but since you think Mr. Prior will be very useful at this time, I will comply with your desire."[1]

Prior was told that above all else he must secure the South American concession from the French. For a while it looked as though he might fail. The French Foreign Minister, de Torcy, told him flatly that France could not agree to the article in regard to the Spanish trade. " My heart ached extremely," wrote Prior to Harley, " and I was ready to sink, but, recollecting myself, I thought it time to say that if this was to continue a maxim I was very sorry that my coming hither was of no effect, and that I looked upon myself as very unhappy, while I told him with the

[1] *Bath Papers.*

same plainness, *ouvertures de cœur* that it was impossible that peace should be made on any other condition."[1]

The French could not afford to let the discussions founder, and in the end conceded the point. Although Prior's talks, as well as the earlier negotiations, were conducted in the utmost secrecy—and no one knew of the French concession—Harley pushed a Bill through the House of Commons in September 1711 setting up the " Company of Merchants of Great Britain trading to the South Seas and other parts of America." This was the bait that would build up pressure for peace. The new Company moved into the Excise Office at the corner of Threadneedle Street and Bishopsgate, and the College of Heralds produced a coat of arms with the motto, " From Cadiz to the Dawn "—Cadiz being regarded as the last outpost of Europe. Harley, now Earl of Oxford, became the first governor, and his friend Mr. St. John, soon to bear the title Lord Bolingbroke, one of the directors.

At the end of 1711, England published the preliminary draft of her negotiations with the French. A howl of rage went up from the Allies. Not only was it branded as treachery, but the terms were appallingly bad. Marlborough had just completed a campaign which many regarded as the most brilliant of his career. France was on the verge of collapse. Why make concessions to Louis XIV with the day so close at hand when the terms could be dictated? A torrent of protest from the signatory powers flowed in to London. George of Hanover, the eldest son of the Electress Sophia, next in line to the British throne, joined the remonstration, pointing out that " the defences of France are already pierced, and after taking one more fortress the Allies will be in the heart of the Kingdom and can have what terms they will." Harley was adamant. A treaty must be signed. There was only one man in Europe whom the Allies might listen to, and that was Marlborough. But when the Duke was approached, he flatly refused to help.

[1] *Harley Papers.*

Harley consulted his friend and colleague, the brilliant, dissipated Henry St. John. They decided that if the Duke would not co-operate he must be removed from office; furthermore a high-powered publicity campaign must be launched to secure support. From then on, events happened with lightning speed. Marlborough was accused of peculation on fabricated charges and removed from his office of Captain-General; the Duchess of Marlborough was stripped of her emoluments and told that her flat in St. James's Palace was required for another; young Robert Walpole, who had served as Secretary at War, was charged with corruption on trumped-up evidence and sent to the Tower; Jonathan Swift was employed to " write down " the Allies and anybody else who opposed the peace. On the tail of all this, in the early months of 1712, a meeting was held in Utrecht as a final attempt to make the Allies fall in with the British proposals.

Lord Oxford and St. John, who was now Lord Bolingbroke, must have impressed foreigners as a curious pair.[1] Both were beginning to drink heavily, but the alcohol seemed to produce opposite effects. Oxford was more diffuse than ever and found it difficult to attend to business. The Queen complained that occasionally he staggered into her presence, and his friends began to comment on his deterioration. " I have long thought his parts decayed," wrote Erasmus Lewis to Swift. Bolingbroke, on the other hand, seemed to derive energy from his dissipations, and grew bolder and rasher every day. This richly gifted man was a strange contradiction; although he was the most brilliant orator of the day and much admired for his political and philosophical writings, not even his closest friends could find much to say for his character. He was totally unprincipled. His morals probably were no worse than many of his contemporaries, but he loved to boast of his excesses. His companions laughed

---

[1] When Bolingbroke told his father that he had been raised to the Peerage, the latter exclaimed " Ah Harry, I ever said you would be hanged, now I find you will be beheaded."

how he "bragged that in one day he was the happiest man alive, got drunk, harangued the Queen, and at night was put to bed to a beautiful young lady, and tucked up by two of the prettiest young Peers in England, Lord Jersey and Bathurst . . ."[1]

Oxford had turned the Utrecht negotiations over to Boling-broke, but after several months the Allies were no nearer agreement than when they started. As no treaty had been signed, it was not possible to prevent the Allies from embarking on a new spring campaign. The Duke of Ormonde had taken Marl-borough's place and was in command of the British troops in Flanders, as well as large German and Dutch contingents, which were paid jointly by Holland and England. Prince Eugene, as usual, commanded the other wing of the Grand Alliance Army, mainly composed of Austrians and Germans. He hoped, in conjunction with Ormonde, to take the fortress of Le Quesnoy and penetrate far into France. Although Bolingbroke could not stop the campaign there was something else he could do; he could smash the Allies' chance of victory.

Oxford was told his scheme, and approved it; but he left Bolingbroke to carry it out alone. Thus one of the most despic-able acts of treachery in British history was put into motion. First of all, Bolingbroke communicated the Allied plan of battle to the French. Secondly, on May 10th, he sent instructions to Ormonde which are famous in history as the "Restraining Orders." "It is the Queen's positive command to your Grace that you must avoid engaging in any siege, or hazarding a battle, till you have further orders from Her Majesty." Ormonde was told not to reveal this order to the Allies; simply to make excuses. After several weeks he sent desperate messages to Harley saying that he had used all the delaying tactics he could think of, and that Prince Eugene was beginning to suspect him. Harley refused to reply. Now Bolingbroke delivered his final

[1] *Prose Works*: Jonathan Swift.

stroke. He came out in the open and announced a truce between the British and French.

It was a stunning blow. The reader must remember that the Allied army believed that the final defeat of France was at hand; that this campaign, pressed with vigour, could bring the long years of war to a glorious and conclusive victory. Instead, Ormonde's troops quit the field. "... the British Army, hitherto the most forward in the Allied cause and admired by all, marched away from the camp of the Allies in bitter humiliation and amid the curses of their old comrades. Only a handful of the British-paid Allies would go with them. Although deprived of their pay and arrears, the great majority declared they would fight on for the "common cause." Many of Marlborough's veterans flung themselves on the ground in shame and fury. The outraged Dutch closed the gates of their cities in the face of the deserting ally. Villars, advancing rapidly, fell upon Eugene's magazines at Denain and inflicted upon him a cruel defeat in which many of his troops were driven into the Scheldt and drowned. Upon this collapse Villars captured all the advanced bases of the Allies and took Douai, Le Quesnoy, and Bouchain. Thus he obliterated the successes of the past three years, and at the end of the terrible war emerged victorious. The English army, under Ormonde, in virtue of a military convention signed with France, retreated upon Dunkirk, which was temporarily delivered to them. After these shattering defeats all the states of the Grand Alliance were compelled to make peace on the best terms possible."[1]

Bolingbroke, far from being ashamed at his Restraining Order, wrote exultingly to Prior in September, " I will not say this order saved their army (the French) from being beat, but I think in my conscience it did." At any rate, he had secured the peace he wanted. The Treaty of Utrecht, a series of agreements between the Allies and France and Spain, was signed in 1713.

[1] *A History of the English Speaking Peoples*: Winston S. Churchill, Cassells.

Years later the great Lord Chatham denounced Utrecht as " an indelible blot on the age."

For Oxford and Bolingbroke, the Treaty had one profound disadvantage. It had deeply offended the Electress Sophia and her son, George, who felt that Hanover had received a shabby deal. If the Crown passed to this family, as Parliament had decreed, the two conspirators would have little chance of office. As a result they began to put out feelers to the Jacobite Court in France. They hinted that if James II's son, the " Prince of Wales " renounced Roman Catholicism, it might be possible to repeal the Act of Settlement and give him the Crown. The Prince, however, replied that nothing would induce him to relinquish his religion, and Oxford realised that this alternative route was no longer open. Bolingbroke, however, continued to keep in close touch with the Jacobites and rumours spread that the Queen was behind him, and would like to see her brother succeed to the throne.

At this point, the rivalry between Oxford and Bolingbroke began to develop into hostility. Once again Abigail played a leading part. She quarrelled with Oxford because he refused to give her " a job of some money out of the Assiento contracts." She told him angrily that she would carry no more messages from him to her mistress. " You never did the Queen any service, nor are you capable of doing her any."[1] What she meant, of course, was that he was slow in doing herself any service. Bolingbroke was much more generous. He raided the secret service funds and bribed her handsomely. Oxford discovered what was going on and his hatred of his old colleague swelled to new proportions.

But Abigail won the day. Although Anne was ill and dispirited, her Lady of the Bedchamber continued to feed her with malicious tittle-tattle, and urged her daily to dismiss Oxford. Finally, on July 27th, 1714, the Queen summoned the two rivals to her presence, and asked Oxford to relinquish the White Staff.

[1] *Prose Works*: Jonathan Swift.

George I, who became Governor of the Company in 1718

The Prince of Wales, Deputy-Governor of the South Sea Company until his breach with the King in 1718

In his fury he shouted at Bolingbroke calling him a liar and a thief. The Queen was so deeply upset by the scene that she took to her bed. Bolingbroke enjoyed only two days of power, for the Queen never rose again. On the 30th, scarcely conscious, she was induced by her Privy Council to hand the White Staff to the Duke of Shrewsbury. Erasmus Lewis reflected the feeling of the assembly when he wrote that Bolingbroke's character was " too bad to carry the great ensigns." The next day the Queen died.

I

THE COURT AND THE COMPANY

" LOOK AT that mawkin and think of her being my son's mistress,"
exclaimed the Electress Sophia. This was some years before the
son in question became George I of England. Yet in September,
1714, when the fifty-four year old Hanoverian prince sailed
across the North Sea to occupy his new throne, the same lady was
still the royal favourite. Her name was the Baroness Ermengarda
Melusina von der Schulenburg. She was peculiarly charmless
with neither wit nor grace to make up for her lack of physical
allure. Tall and bony and wooden, the English nick-named her
" The Maypole." Only George could see her magic. " His
mistress " wrote Lord Chesterfield, " with whom he passed most
of his time and who held all influence over him, was little better
than an idiot."[1] However, the courtiers and statesmen of the day
soon realised how important it was to ingratiate themselves with
the lady and received good value for their efforts. Years later Sir
Robert Walpole confided that he did " everything by her ";
that she was in effect " as much Queen of England as ever any
was."

Both George and his mistress took up residence in London
with a marked lack of enthusiasm. The Baroness had been told
that the English treated their kings barbarously and was convinced that her lover's head would be chopped off in a fortnight.
She was so terrified at being involved in his " ruin " that she
refused to join him for some months. George was equally reluctant to quit his native land but for different reasons. Whereas
his mother, the shrewd, quick-witted Electress, had longed to
wear the English crown, George regarded it as an unenviable

[1] *Characters*: Lord Chesterfield.

34

duty. Too big a plum to cast aside, he would have been just as happy if it had dropped into someone else's lap. The truth was that he adored Hanover. Totally unimaginative and totally unambitious, he had no desire to play a role upon a larger stage. In his electorate he was absolute ruler; he was rich, envied, even admired. He was proud of his large country estate at Herrenhausen, and found the bourgeois routine of his petty court agreeable and satisfying. His chief sport was hunting and his chief pleasure over-eating.

George revealed his reluctance to assume his new duties by delaying his departure for England until a month after Queen Anne's death; and in a speech to his principality he made it clear that he was not going for good. " Farewell, dear place, where I have spent so many happy and peaceful hours; I leave you but not for ever, for I shall hope to see you again frequently." He travelled to Holland and embarked at Orange Polder on the yacht *Peregrine*. He was accompanied by his son, soon to be created Prince of Wales, and a company of one hundred Hanoverians, ranging from ministers, courtiers, cooks and trumpeters to two Turkish valets, Mustapha and Mahomet, whom he had captured in a campaign in Hungary thirty years before. The royal conclave arrived at Greenwich on September 18th, and was greeted with great pomp and ceremony. The poets outdid themselves in laudatory odes to the King; one eulogy began, " Oh great Brunswick! " and described the monarch as

> *Mature in wisdom, his extensive mind*
> *Takes in the blended interests of mankind . . .*

Unfortunately the extensive mind had never taken in the language of his new subjects. George could not speak a word of English. It seems extraordinary that the Electress, who was so proud of being half English, had neglected this facet of her son's education. She had taught him the diplomatic language, French, and some Italian, but that was all. As a boy he had not dreamt that one day he would be called upon to rule England and when the Act of Settlement of 1701 fixed the House of Hanover in the line of succession, George was forty-one, and declared himself too old to learn a new tongue. Two months after his arrival in England his cousin, the Duchesse d'Orléans, better known in history as " Madame," wrote to a relation, " I do not believe that the English, who are so impatient, will put up for any time with a king who cannot speak the language." However, Madame did not assess the situation correctly. The Whig oligarchy had not chosen George for his accomplishments, or even because they liked him. They needed him to ensure the Protestant Succession.

Many of them were glad of his failings for they saw an opportunity to wrest power from the Crown; and in this they were not mistaken. George had no desire to involve himself in English quarrels or to assume any unnecessary responsibility. He had only one stipulation to make; that his Government should be composed entirely of Whigs. He loathed the Tories, not only because of their Jacobite tendencies, but because they were responsible for the Treaty of Utrecht which had prevented his beloved German states from exacting reparations from the French. George made up his mind to appoint an all-Whig government, then to sit back and play the role of a figurehead. His ministers could make decisions in his name. " Then," he announced cheerfully, " they will be responsible for everything I do."

Things did not work out as easily as George hoped, for his reign is memorable for only one thing: the greatest financial scandal of the age. As he himself was destined to become involved in this affair, let us take a closer look at his character. " The King," declared an English wit, " was undoubtedly of an affectionate nature for of all the people in the world he hated only three: his mother, his wife and his son."

Probably it was an exaggeration to say that George hated his mother, but he left no doubt as to his feelings for wife and son. The wife had earned his wrath by making the mistake, twelve years after marriage, of falling in love with a dashing young Swedish count. George returned from the wars to be confronted by a packet of love letters—handed him by a malevolent courtier —which he interpreted as proof of her guilt. In the meantime the lover had disappeared and was never heard of again; murdered, the story went, on orders from a jealous and ageing ex-mistress, the Countess of Platen. George divorced his wife and deprived her of her two children—an eleven year old boy who was to become George II, and a ten year old daughter who was to marry the King of Prussia. Then he packed her off to a dreary castle in the north of Germany for the rest of her life; indeed, she was still languishing there in misery and isolation.

After his wife's disgrace, George could not bear the sight of his son. Some people said that he did not believe the child to be his own; others claimed that the boy had tried to intervene on his mother's behalf. Whatever the truth, deep animosity smouldered between the two throughout their lives.

George's harsh treatment of his wife prompted most Europeans to regard him as a cold, vindictive martinet. The English, however, were inclined to look upon him merely as a simpleton. " The King's character," commented the celebrated traveller and letter writer, Lady Mary Wortley Montagu, " may be comprised in a very few words. In private life he would have been called an honest block-head . . ." This judgement was partly due to the King's inability to speak English. He was not a clever man and his linguistic shortcomings made him appear even stupider. Officially, the difficulties that confronted him were not insurmountable. The Lord Chancellor read the King's speeches to Parliament, and the King's ministers struggled to write their reports in French so their master could understand them. When this became too laborious, German advisors were called in to translate. Robert Walpole read French but apparently did not speak it fluently for he boasted that he controlled the King " by bad Latin and good punch."

Socially, the language barrier was far more formidable.

Many of the richest and haughtiest nobles could not speak any tongue but their own. They found it humiliating not to be able to communicate with their sovereign, and blamed him rather than themselves. Although George loathed ceremonials and severely curtailed his public appearances, his advisors insisted that he hold three Drawing Rooms a week at St. James's Palace. These proved a trial for everyone. More than one guest tried to melt into the background, as the monarch approached, to avoid the ordeal of a conversation. Once he bore down on the Duchess of Bolton who had just come from the theatre where she had seen Cibber's comedy, *Love's Last Shift.* "And what was the name of your play?" asked the King affably. The Duchess could not think how to put it in French. Finally she stammered, "*La Dernière Chemise de l'Amour.*"

Needless to say, George did not find his new subjects any more entertaining than they found him. He could only relax with his own compatriots. "The King has no predilection for the English nation," the French ambassador reported, "and never receives in private any English of either sex, none even of his principal officers are invited to his chamber in the morning to dress him nor in the evening to undress him. These offices are performed by the Turks who are his *valets de chambre* and who give him every thing he wants in private . . ." The King spent most of his evenings with the Baroness Schulenburg, smoking and drinking beer. She entertained him, hour after hour, by cutting paper into odd shapes. When this diversion palled, he sometimes went to the apartment of Madame Kielmansegge. This lady, the gossips claimed, was a secondary mistress. Whatever her relationship, it was clear that although George was fond of her, she did not exercise the same hold over him as the Baroness. Lady Mary Wortley Montagu insists that she was "very agreeable in her person when adorned with youth" but she was nearly fifty when she came to England, and immensely fat. "I remember as a boy being terrified at her enormous figure," wrote Horace Walpole. "The fierce black eyes, large and rolling beneath two lofty arched eyebrows, two acres of cheeks spread with crimson, an ocean of neck, that over-flowed, and was not distinguished from the lower part of her body, and no part restrained by stays. No wonder that a child dreaded such an ogress."[1]

Sometimes the King took the two women driving in his carriage. Madame Schulenburg was already "The Maypole" and Madame Kielmansegge soon became "The Elephant." These outings did not increase George's popularity. The lower orders expected their King to have mistresses, but not ugly ones. The royal carriage was often greeted with whistles and coarse laughter, sometimes even boos.

The aristocracy was more polite. They showed the favourites every civility but made jokes behind their backs. The quips were repeated back to Hanover and caused great anger among the ladies of the Court who felt that their personal honour was at stake. They lost no chance to retaliate with disparaging remarks, and soon a female slanging match had developed between the two countries. Lady Cowper, the wife of one of George's ministers, became the chief reporter of this sort of tittle-tattle. "The Countess of Buckenburg said, in a visit," she wrote in her diary, "that the English women did not look like women of quality, but made themselves look as pitifully and sneakingly as they could; that they hold their heads down, and look always in a fright, whereas those that are forignors hold up their heads and hold out their breasts, and make themselves look as great and stately as they can, and more nobly and more like quality than the others. To which Lady Deloraine replied, 'We show our quality by our birth and titles, Madam, not by sticking out our bosoms.'"

The King had not been in England long, before his attention was called to the South Sea Company. This four year old concern enjoyed immense prestige but it lacked the golden touch.

[1] *Reminiscences of the Courts of George I and II*: Horace Walpole.

Although its foundations had helped to promote peace with Spain, the Spanish King, Philip V, had not displayed the generosity that Lord Oxford had envisaged. He refused to allow the Company to send more than one cargo of merchandise a year to his subjects in South America, and even from this slim venture, insisted on a share of the profits. The only concession he willingly granted was the *Assiento*—permission to transport negro slaves to the South American plantations. But this contract proved to be fraught with dangers. The sea voyages from Africa were long and costly, and many of the negroes died on the way. Furthermore the unarmed ships were sometimes attacked by buccaneers, and sometimes driven away by Spanish *costa guarda* vessels who claimed that they had received no " instructions " from Madrid to let them land. Lastly there was much illegal competition. English privateers had been doing a lucrative business in slave-trading for years, and despite the South Sea monopoly, refused to give it up. They smuggled thousands of negroes to the plantations, often exhausting the South Sea quota and spoiling the market.

On top of these difficulties, the Company had received a further blow by losing its two most important directors. Lord Bolingbroke had been frightened by rumours that he was to be imprisoned for treason and had skipped off to France. Lord Oxford stood his ground, and discovered that the rumours were true. In 1715 he was sent to the Tower to await trial. Luckily for him, he was kept waiting so long that when his case finally was heard, emotions had died and no charges were brought against him. He spent the remainder of his life in retirement in the country.

The directors of the South Sea Company were eager to interest the King in their affairs, in the hope that he might secure them better terms from the King of Spain. At this stage George had no wish to embroil himself in English business affairs, and showed little enthusiasm. The best the Company could do was to persuade the Prince of Wales to become a shareholder and to name its first ship after him.[1] The launching took place in 1715, and the Prince and his retinue attended the ceremony in person.

How was it possible that this highly respectable, if slightly unlucky, Company was soon to involve the King, and the King's mistresses, ministers and M.P.s, in sensational happenings that not only would threaten the Government but rock the throne itself? In 1715 the pattern was not discernible, yet the main strands were on the loom. And the most important thread was the rapaciousness of Madame Schulenburg.

The German entourage was dazzled by the wealth of England and determined to get a share of it. Although the English were horrified by the size of the national debt, and grumbled endlessly about taxation, no foreigner could visit Britain without being impressed by its affluence. The standard of living was higher than in any other country in the world, and its benefits permeated to all classes of society. " Even servant-maids wear silks on Sundays and holidays, when they are almost as well dressed as their mistresses," commented a French tourist. "Even those we call poor people . . . lye warm, live in plenty, work hard and (need) know no want," wrote Daniel Defoe.

The national wealth came from two sources—the lush land which supported a population of little more than five million, and the prosperous trade with India and Africa. But private wealth sprang from a variety of ventures. The aristocracy as well as the merchants, had a craze for business. They invested their money in every sort of enterprise, ranging from building projects, mines and real estate to water-works, shipping, coal and copper. Many great nobles amassed fortunes by marrying their sons to daughters of great merchants; others simply from holding government offices. The Duke of Chandos was said to have collected £300,000 from being Paymaster of the Forces during Marlborough's wars; and the Earl of Nottingham made £50,000 in six years as a Secretary of State. Their wealth permeated every

[1] Up until now the Company had chartered ships.

class of society for no aristocracy in Europe spent money more freely or lived in greater splendour.

A noble with an income of £5,000 (although the purchasing power of the pound was many times what it is to-day) was not considered well off. The Dukes of Bedford, Marlborough, Buckingham, Montagu and Chandos had incomes in the region of £50,000 a year. These men not only owned large houses in London but built themselves palaces in the country as well—an eccentric habit which was copied by rich merchants and grew increasingly prevalent and increasingly English as the century progressed. The country seats were spared no expense. The Duke of Chandos, for instance, spent £200,000 building Cannons at Little Stanmore in Middlesex. " Europe has nothing to compare with it," wrote Daniel Defoe in awed tones. The Duke had a full orchestra to play during meals and the household staff numbered ninety-three. He was very proud of his collection of exotic birds. In his aviaries were " whistling owls and flamingoes from Antigua . . . blue macaws and geese; Muscovy ducks, Virginia fowls and song-birds; a Gold Coast redbird of peculiar prettiness; Barbadoes ' Powises ' and parakeets, an eagle, and a crown bird."[1]

A number of well-connected English travellers made a speciality of trying to stimulate the appetites of the dukes. One of these wanderers, John Russell, concentrated on the Duke of Bedford. He tried to interest him in black boys and monkeys without success. Then he made another suggestion to which the Duke replied briefly: " I return you many thanks for the offer of the Tiger, but do not care to concern myself with any of these sort of animals." In the end Russell scored a triumph for the next year the Duke's steward was writing: " I received the Turtle and well in health. His Grace was afraid it would not come. His Grace had about twelve ladies and gentlemen at the eating of it. We dressed it after the West India manner and the Duke said he never ate a better in his life. His Grace said he hoped he

[1] *Chandos*: Colin Baker and Muriel Baker.

should get another this year, but could not tell. He should be glad if he could, for he loves them exceedingly. The goose and cocoa nuts I shall have tonight . . ."[1]

Although the lesser nobles could not compete with the ducal establishments, they did not live badly. " We used to sit down to dinner," wrote the Duchess of Marlborough's friend, Lord Hervey of Houghton, " a little snug party of about thirty odd, up to the chin in beef, venison, geese, turkeys, etc.; and the Lords Spiritual and Temporal, besides commoners, parsons and free-holders innumerable." The custom of feeding the neighbours for miles around could prove ruinously expensive. " A curious fact is that many noblemen live in town to economize," commented Monsieur de Saussure, " and though they are surrounded with great luxury, they declare that in their country seats they are forced to spend far more, having to keep open house and table, packs of hounds, stables full of horses, and to entertain followers of every description. When in town they do not have these same expenses, but they are not so much thought of as in the country where they are like little kings . . ."[2]

Surrounded by vast wealth and prolific spending, it is small wonder that Madame Schulenburg in particular, and the German followers in general, had hopes of lining their purses and acquiring a few titles. Philip Stanhope, a nineteenth-century historian, describes them as " a flight of hungry Hanoverians who like so many famished vultures fell with keen eyes and bended talons on the fruitful soil of England." However, they did not find the way easy. To their surprise and chagrin they discovered that a passage in the Act of Settlement of 1701 barred them from accepting titles or " positions of profit " under the Crown. This clause had been slipped in because of the disapproval aroused when William of Orange freely dispensed honours to the Dutch followers. Madame Schulenburg thought she saw a way round

[1] *A Forgotten John Russell*: E. Matcham.
[2] *A Foreign View of England*: César de Saussure.

the regulation and became naturalised. She pressed the King for a title and he discussed the matter with Lord Townshend. Townshend apparently did not fully appreciate the extent of Madame's influence, for he pointed out that the Act specifically debarred " strangers though naturalised." He said he would do his best and the following year informed the King that he had arranged for Madame Schulenburg to have an Irish title, and become the Duchess of Munster. The favourite was very angry. She was certain an English title could have been produced if Townshend had thrown his heart into it, and from that moment on resolved to destroy his influence with the King.

Despite her disappointment, her rival Madame Kielmansegge, who had received nothing, was " mightily mortified." This lady was visiting Hanover at the time, and an English resident by the name of Mr. Clavering, wrote to Lady Cowper, " You must know we have two parties here more violent than Whig and Tory in England (which are the Schulenburg and Kielmansegge factions). Madame Kielmansegge is very unwilling to give place to the new duchess; therefore she will petition Parliament to be naturalised, that she may have a title equal to the other."[1] But Madame Kielmansegge had to wait many years; in 1722 she was given a title, but no higher than the rank of Countess.

The new Duchess of Munster was not content merely with a title; she wanted money to go with it. Although she could not hold a position of profit, she was quick to see that all power sprang from the King, in view of his absolute control of a huge patronage. Why not make his subjects pay for their lucrative appointments? The Duchess was not the only member of his intimate circle to come to this conclusion; most of the courtiers and the two Turkish valets saw innumerable ways to line their purses, and were soon doing a profitable trade.

The Duchess proved the most efficient. First of all, when the Master of the Horse, the Duke of Somerset, resigned in 1716, she persuaded the King not to appoint anyone in his place but to

[1] *Diary*: Lady Cowper.

let her draw the emoluments of £7,500 a year. This provided a steady basis from which she could operate. She scored plenty of coups. She sold the patent of the copper coinage in Ireland for £14,000; she made even larger sums by securing peerages for important persons; and some years later was said to have mulcted Lord Bolingbroke of £11,000 in return for a pardon from the King. Sir Robert Walpole remarked that she " would have sold the King's honour for a shilling advance to the highest bidder." However this plainly was not necessary.

The avariciousness of the German followers became common gossip and exaggerated stories were repeated in taverns and coffee houses. When the King took the Duchess driving in his carriage the jeers were louder than ever. Once she leaned out of the window to remonstrate with the hecklers in her broken English. " Goot people vy do you reproach us? Ve come for all your goots." " Yes," cried a voice, " and for our chattels too."

This story may be apocryphal, but it could be true. The lower classes were independent and aggressive. Their lack of servility, and uninhibited dealings with their betters struck visitors as amazing. " The insolence of the populace is so great," wrote M. de Saussure, " that as soon as an honest man has any disagreement with one of their kind, he is at once invited to strip and fight with the fists. It would be dangerous to retaliate with a cane or sword; the lookers-on would at once be against him, and things might end badly for him. Noblemen of rank, almost beside themselves with anger at the arrogance of a carter or person of that sort, have been seen to throw off their coats, wigs, and swords, in order to use their fists. This sort of adventure often befell the Duke of Leeds, and he even made it into an amusement. My Lord Herbert, who is a very strong and robust man, recently fought a porter, and punished him well; the man was so surprised that he exclaimed, ' D—— sure you are the son of a porter, not of a lord; you know how to use your fists too well.' "[1]

[1] *A Foreign View of England:* César de Saussure.

On public occasions, such as the Lord Mayor's Day, the crowds were even more bellicose. " At these times it is almost dangerous for an honest man, and more particularly for a foreigner, if at all well dressed, to walk in the streets, for he runs a great risk of being insulted by the vulgar populace,which is the most cursed brood in existence. He is sure of not only being jeered at and being bespattered with mud, but as likely as not dead dogs and cats will be thrown at him, for the mob makes a provision beforehand of these playthings, so that they may amuse themselves with them on the great day. If the stranger were to get angry, his treatment would be all the worse. The best thing to be done on these occasions is not to run the risk of mixing with the crowd; but, should you desire to do so from curiosity, you had better dress yourself as simply as possible in the English fashion, and trust to pass unnoticed. I daresay it would interest you to hear of the style and the way Englishmen usually dress. They do not trouble themselves about dress, but leave that to their women-folk. When the people see a well-dressed person in the streets, especially if he is wearing a braided coat, a plume in his hat, or his hair tied in a bow, he will, without doubt, be called ' French dog' twenty times perhaps before he reaches his destination. This name is the most common, and evidently, according to popular idea, the greatest and most forcible insult that can be given to any man, and it is applied indifferently to all foreigners, French or otherwise. Englishmen are usually very plainly dressed, they scarcely ever wear gold on their clothes; they wear little coats called ' frocks,' without facings and without pleats, with a short cape above. Almost all wear small, round wigs, plain hats, and carry canes in their hands, but no swords. Their cloth and linen are of the best and finest. You will see rich merchants and gentlemen thus dressed, and sometimes even noblemen of high rank, especially in the morning, walking through the filthy and muddy streets. Englishmen are, however, very lavish in other ways. They have splendid equipages and costly apparel when required. Peers and other persons of rank are richly dressed when they go to Court, especially on gala days, when their grand coaches, with their magnificent accoutrements, are used. The lower classes are usually well dressed, wearing good cloth and linen. You never see wooden shoes in England, and the poorest individuals never go with naked feet."[1]

Unwittingly, the Duchess of Munster selected the cast for the South Sea drama. Her rapaciousness caused a major Cabinet reshuffle, and a number of statesmen suddenly were thrust into roles they otherwise would not have played. The upheaval occurred because the Duchess was still determined to acquire an English title, and blamed Lord Townshend for not presenting her with one. The Earl of Sunderland—the same gentleman who had been such a controversial figure in Queen Anne's reign—managed to scrape an acquaintance with the favourite, and assured her that if she could persuade the King to make him first minister in Lord Townshend's place, he would repeal the relevant clauses in the Act of Settlement, and make her an English duchess. From this moment on, the lady's course was clear.

In the eighteenth century, politicians had a tendency to operate in pairs. Townshend's running mate was his childhood friend, Robert Walpole. Townshend had been a ward of Walpole's father, a well-to-do Norfolk squire, and when Robert, who was a few years his junior, came to London, Townshend made him a member of the famous Whig Kit Kat Club and introduced him to the most fashionable circle of the day. Walpole presented a slightly comic figure. His face was round and pink-cheeked, and he weighed nearly twenty stone. He looked like an over-size cherub, and an Eton education had not managed to supply him with any polish. "Inelegant in his manners, loose in his morals, he had a coarse strong wit, which he was too free of for a man in his station," wrote Lord Chesterfield. However, it probably was this very wit and vitality that soon made him a

[1] *A Foreign View of England:* César de Saussure.

figure in society. A few years later, when he was married, his sister Dolly was thrilled to visit him in London. She was twenty years old, " a beautiful, innocent well-meaning girl, but endowed only with a portion of sense." Dolly immediately got mixed up with the most notorious libertine of the day, Lord Wharton, and when Mrs. Walpole tried to make her stop seeing him, she packed her bags and left. She took refuge with Lady Wharton. This may seem odd but Lady Wharton made a habit of befriending her husband's victims. Robert went in pursuit of her and ordered her out of the house. Charles Townshend helped by inviting her to stay with him and his wife until Robert could arrange to send her back to Norfolk. A few years later Lady Townshend died, and Lord Townshend married Dolly. Thus the ties between the two men were drawn tighter than ever.

When Townshend became George's first minister, no one was surprised to see him install his brother-in-law, first as Paymaster of the Forces, then as Chancellor of the Exchequer. Walpole was delighted with both jobs. He was badly in need of money and the office of Paymaster was notoriously profitable. This minister was allowed to invest the large revenues at his disposal, and keep the interest for himself. Although Walpole's father had left him an income of £2,000 a year from his estates, and Mrs. Walpole had money of her own, Robert was always in debt. He spent money like water, demanding the best food and wines and trying to compete with the aristocracy in the luxury with which he ran his country house. For several years he had held a minor job at the Admiralty and had managed to make a bit of money on the side, importing wines and laces from Holland and smuggling them into England duty free. This was a risky business but Walpole pulled it off by commandeering an Admiralty yacht. The idea of cheating the Government he was serving did not strike him as the least odd; many other people did it, and boasted of their successes quite openly in letters.

Meanwhile the high-handed, unscrupulous Earl of Sunderland viewed the Townshend-Walpole partnership with open distaste.

Madame Schulenburg, Duchess of Kendal, known as "the Maypole." Mistress of George I, she received a large parcel of South Sea stock in return for her support

Baroness von Kielmansegge, another favourite of George I, known as "the Elephant"

He had been fobbed off with a minor ministerial job, and decided that the only way to secure promotion was to ingratiate himself with the sovereign. When the King went to Hanover on a visit, the Earl departed for Aix-les-Bains, on a pretext of health. His friend—and political running mate—Lord Stanhope was a member of the royal entourage, and managed to use Sunderland's proximity as an excuse for inviting him to join the King at a shooting party near Frankfurt. And Sunderland made himself irresistible. He charmed George so completely that he laid the foundations of a lasting friendship. He also plotted with the Duchess. Together they criticised Townshend's handling of foreign affairs, seizing every opportunity to draw the King's attention to the fact that his policy towards Sweden showed a callous indifference to the interests of the German states.

This line of attack was successful. Early in 1717 Townshend was curtly dismissed, and Walpole, who had become First Lord of the Treasury and Chancellor of the Exchequer, felt himself obliged to resign in protest. The two Earls—Sunderland and Stanhope—were now supreme; and the Irish Duchess of Munster was informed that she soon would become the English Duchess of Kendal.

Walpole was sad to lose his high office. He had shown himself a shrewd and able Chancellor and considered the turn in his fortunes most unlucky. He could not know that the Duchess's machinations, which had forced him to leave the Government, had, at the same time, cast him as the hero of the South Sea drama.

Now all the characters, save one, had assumed their roles. Only the King was left to take up his part. The South Sea Company was still trying to interest him in its affairs. Indeed it had almost become a matter of urgent necessity, for nothing seemed to be going right. The Company's first ship did not sail until 1717 and by the time it reached South America a short fierce war had broken out between Britain and Spain and the vessel had no option but to return home.[1] The Company now invited George to become its Governor. The Prince of Wales was a shareholder and would have liked this office himself, but his name was reserved as Deputy Governor until the King made up his mind.

George was more inclined to listen to the Company's proposals now than before. He was deeply in debt for he had overspent the allowance granted him by Parliament by hundreds of thousands of pounds. True the South Sea Company had met with little success; but the directors argued that with his patronage their difficulties would be overcome and promised him a large share of the profits.

The King hesitated for some time, chiefly because he did not want to serve on the same board with the Prince. Then a fantastic episode occurred, which not only removed this particular obstacle, but set every tongue in Europe wagging. The smouldering animosity between the King and his son exploded into a bitter quarrel. The Prince was thirty-five years old, a diminutive, strutting peacock with a vile temper. He loved pageantry as much as his father hated it and fancied himself as an irresistible figure in society. He had an asset in his attractive blonde, quick-witted wife, a German princess, Caroline of Anspach. Unlike her husband she had the advantage of speaking fluent English. This, coupled with high spirits and sharp intellect, won her many admirers although some people criticised her for being too aggressive and loquacious. When later she was on the throne a malicious poet composed a ballad which began:

> *Since England was England, there never was seen*
> *So strutting a King or so prating a Queen . . .*

On the whole, however, she escaped criticism and even managed to get on reasonably with her father-in-law, although he

---

[1] The Company of course, had chartered a good many ships to carry slaves from Africa to South America under the terms of the Assiento but these voyages had not proved profitable.

occasionally referred to her as "*Cette diablesse, Madame la Princesse.*"

The Princess had the unenviable lot of living with her father-in-law. She and her husband and three daughters were given suites in St. James's Palace, where George could supervise their movements. He interfered in almost everything they did. He appointed the people who served them, criticised their behaviour, and kept tight control over their children. He refused to allow their eldest son, Frederick, to join them in England, insisting that the boy should be educated in Hanover. This was odd considering the difficulties created by his own ignorance of language and people. The Princess possessed great tact and managed the difficult situation with admirable coolness

Then came the event that ruptured the relationship. In November, 1717, she gave birth to her fifth child and second son. The christening took place in the Chapel Royal, St. James's, in February. The Prince and Princess selected two royalties (apart from the King) to stand as godparents to the child; the Queen of Prussia and the Duke of York. However, the King in his customary high-handed way made his own selection and apparently did not bother to inform his son. He chose commoners: the Duke of Newcastle and the Duchess of St. Albans. The King attended the ceremonies and the christening began pleasantly enough. The Prince was under the impression that Newcastle and the Duchess were present to stand proxy for the royal sponsors. When the crucial moment came, and to his amazement he heard the Bishop naming the unroyal pair as godparents, his fury knew no bounds. He moved forward and whispered in the Duke's ear, "You rascal, I fight you."

The Duke reported this to the King and now it was George's turn to be transported by rage. He sent three dukes (Kingston, Kent and Roxburgh) to his son, bearing an order in his own writing, to find out exactly what had happened. The Prince replied that he had not said "I fight you" but "I find you," meaning "I find you out." The King was not impressed and ordered the Prince and Princess to leave the Palace that very day. They were forbidden to take their children with them; and a message was sent to the Captain General of the Forces (the Duke of Marlborough) to withdraw horse and footguards from their entourage. Lord Grantham was brave enough to give the unfortunate couple refuge in his house in Albemarle Street until they found a place of their own. The poor Princess was in tears at being parted from her children. She was not to see them again for several years; and a few weeks later she had the added grief of learning that her newly born son had died. The ballad writers of the day were not distinguished for their good taste and verses were circulated describing the royal quarrel and ending with the lines:

> *Now Sire and Son had played their part,*
> *What could befall beside?*
> *Why the poor babe took this to heart,*
> *Kicked up its heels and died.*

George's vengeance did not stop with the children. He heard that Lord Grantham was trying to acquire the Duke of Ormonde's house at Richmond for the Prince, and sent word to him that if the arrangements went through he would seize the property as being forfeit to the Crown. He sent messages to the theatres forbidding their actors to perform before the Prince. He made it clear that persons visiting the Heir Apparent would have to reckon with his disapproval. He even wrote to foreign courts notifying them of his son's disgrace.

The Prince had an income of £50,000 from the Civil List; and Parliament, whose sympathy had been aroused, infuriated the King by voting him another £50,000 a year. He was able to buy a large house in Leicester Square—then known as Leicester Fields—and set up a rival court. The Tory opposition had nothing to lose by attending his levees, and soon he had a large and lively circle of dissidents.

The quarrel was the sensation of Europe. Every court on the Continent buzzed with gossip and watched developments in London with fascinated interest. George's desire to torment the Heir Apparent seemed insatiable. People whispered that he had written a will depriving the Prince of his Hanover inheritance but this document never came to light. (Some said it was burnt by the Prince when his father died.) Another act was to approve a peerage Bill which would have limited the monarch's right to create peers.[1] This was an extraordinary case of cutting off the nose to spite the face. Although it would have curtailed his own powers, the King was persuaded to support it in order to lessen the authority of his son upon his succession.

He did something else. He accepted the invitation of the South Sea Company to become Governor, and struck off the name of the Prince as Deputy Governor. " You remember when the South Sea brat was said to be Lord Oxford's brat," wrote the Duchess of Ormonde to Swift. " Now the King has adopted it and calls it ' his beloved child '; though perhaps you may say, if he loves it no better than his son it may not be saying much. But he loves it as much as he loves the Duchess of Kendal and that is saying a great deal."

[1] This Bill was defeated in the House of Commons, and never became law.

II

MR. LAW AND THE
MISSISSIPPI BOOM

IF IT had not been for a series of extraordinary events in France the South Sea Company might have jogged on indefinitely as a respectable failure, living on the annual interest paid to it by the Government for having taken over £10,000,000 of debts upon its foundation. Unmeaningly the French staged a dress rehearsal for the South Sea drama; more than this, the Paris performance introduced a novel twist which fired the imagination of the English directors.

Oddly enough, the chief actor in the French production was a British subject by the name of Mr. John Law. "I must say I saw nothing in France that delighted me so much as to see an Englishman (or at least a Briton) absolute in Paris," wrote Lady Mary Wortley Montagu in 1718. "I mean Mr. Law, who treats the Dukes and Peers extremely *de haut en bas* and is treated by them with the utmost submission and respect."

Mr. Law was a fascinating Scottish adventurer who had settled in Paris in 1713. Two years later the great King had died. The new King, Louis XV, was only five years old, and France was ruled by a Regent—the forty-one year old Duc d'Orléans—a nephew of Louis XIV. The task that confronted the Duke was appalling. The English grumbled about their war debts, but France was tottering on the brink of bankruptcy. Worse still, it was demoralised.

There were no clever men to step forward and pull it back from the precipice. Louis XIV had ruled for over fifty years as an absolute dictator. When he was a child the nobles had revolted against the Crown in a civil war known as the Fronde. He had never forgiven them, and years later, he employed original and artful means to destroy them as a ruling class. He had created Versailles and established it as the centre of the universe. It was run like a huge house-party. All the greatest and most fashionable aristocrats revolved around the court; those who remained on their estates were ridiculed as dowdy and provincial. They became so addicted to the pleasures of hunting, eating, drinking and womanizing that far from resisting the King's will they were delighted to have someone organising the tiresome details of life for them.

The Regent was a clever, liberal-minded man, but he, too, suffered from the weaknesses of the flesh. Although he had shown intellectual promise as a boy, and displayed talent for both music and science, these pursuits had long been dimmed by an insatiable desire for women and drink. His orgies at the Palais Royal became famous. His group was small and select and enlivened by actresses and courtesans. Every night the doors were locked, no servants were permitted to enter, and the revelry went on until the small hours of the morning. His mother—a first cousin of George I—was horrified. "My son is no longer a youth of twenty, he is a man of forty-one years of age, so Paris cannot forgive him for running off to balls after women in such a hair-brained fashion when he has all the affairs of State on his shoulders" she wrote to the Princess of Wales. "When the late King came into possession of his throne everything was in a prosperous state so it was all right for him to amuse himself, but to-day that isn't at all the case. He should work day and night to repair what the King, or rather, his unfaithful ministers have done."[1]

The Regent, despite his late hours was surprisingly conscientious, and was at his desk every morning at eight o'clock. He had a genuine desire to liberalise the Government, and to restore a number of functions to the Parliament. He also tried to re-endow the nobility with the power that Louis XIV had snatched

[1] *Letters of Madame*: Translated and edited by Gertrude Scott Stevenson.

from it. Instead of secretaries of state, drawn from the middle classes, running the great departments, he set up councils composed entirely of nobles, to take over the task. To his chagrin he found it was too late. The nobles had lost both the taste and the capacity to govern. For example, when he offered the chief position in the council of finance to his close friend, the Duc de Saint-Simon, the latter declined, boasting of his incompetence. He said that commerce, circulation and exchange were known to him hardly by name; he had never mastered even the first rules of arithmetic; he had never taken charge of his private estate, because he knew that he was incapable. If he had control of the finances, though he might not steal himself, his ignorance would allow others to play riot in the treasury. The Regent soon saw that a glorious aristocratic revival was not going to be possible. Gradually he reverted to his uncle's system of autocracy.

But meanwhile who was to solve the appalling problem of France's finances? The nobles threw up their hands in helplessness and suggested declaring a state of national bankruptcy. This would result in widespread misery, yet no one had an alternative. At this point Mr. John Law stepped forward. He was brimming over with ideas and claimed to have a happy solution for France's difficulties. Not only could he stave off bankruptcy, but he could create a prosperity the like of which the country had never seen.

The Regent had met Mr. Law several years before at gambling parties in Paris. His host was Monsieur Duclos, one of the leading actors of the day, and the favourite game was faro. Law was a striking figure. Dark and lean, with aquiline features and exquisite manners, he was much admired by the ladies. He always made a dramatic entrance carrying a bag of gold said to be worth £20,000. He stirred great interest by effecting complete indifference as to whether he won or lost. It must be remembered that gambling was not regarded as a vice in those days. Gentlemen were expected to frequent the card table just as readily as the ballroom, and skill at play was regarded as a high social attainment. The fact that Mr. Law despite his unconcern, usually won, made him an object of adulation. He always replied that his good fortune was due neither to luck nor skill, but to a system. "He had studied the combination of cards to a degree," wrote Saint-Simon, "which to me seemed quite incredible, so that wherever he went he won enormously at play, though he never cheated."

Law bought a luxurious house in the Place Vendôme and entertained generously. His success inspired gossip and soon all sorts of rumours were circulating about him. It was said that he had run off with another man's wife, who was now posing as his own; and that he was wanted in England for murder. Although there is no evidence to prove that Lady Catherine Law, the daughter of the Earl of Banbury, was not really married to him, the murder charge was true.

John Law was the son of an Edinburgh goldsmith. He left home at fourteen, when his father died. He had a small patrimony which he soon spent leaving him only his wits to live on. He was fascinated by figures and made an intensive study of gambling which eventually provided him with a steady income. He was greatly pursued by women, and when he was twenty-six became involved with a certain Mrs. Lawrence. This lady had another lover as well, known as Beau Wilson, who took exception to Law's attentions. An acrimonious correspondence passed between the two men, and one night, when they met accidentally in Bloomsbury Square, they both drew their swords and passed at each other. Wilson died instantly. Law was arrested, tried, and found guilty of murder. After some months, however, he managed to secure a pardon from the Crown; but just when he thought he was going to be released the dead man's brother filed a suit against him and he was incarcerated in the King's Bench Prison. Apparently this was too much for Mr. Law, so he organised a successful escape. A notice appeared in the London Gazette of January declaring that anyone supplying information leading to the arrest of "Captain John Lawe, a

Scotchman lately a prisoner in the King's Bench for murder, aged twenty-six, a very tall, black, lean man well shaped, above six foot high, large pock holes in his face, big high nosed, speaks broad and loud, who made his escape from the said prison, shall have fifty pounds paid immediately by the Marshall of the King's Bench."

Law went abroad and spent the next few years wandering around the capitals of Europe. Soon he had acquired a large fortune gambling and was able to move in the highest circles. His real interest was the theory of banking and company trading. In England he had studied the system of the Bank of England. Now he scrutinised the workings of the banks of Amsterdam and Venice. Gradually he developed a new and striking theory about the meaning and use of money.

When the Regent came to power, Law saw his chance and asked for an interview. He talked French fluently, despite a Scotch accent which was regarded as very droll. He had a plan for France. He expounded it with force and lucidity, and the Regent was deeply impressed. France, he claimed, was a rich, clever and industrious country. Her financial troubles were not inherent, but simply due to a shortage of gold and silver. Gold and silver, he argued, could never be an ideal currency because it was too costly to produce and always in short supply. What was needed was a bank which could create an adequate supply of paper money. Paper money was as superior to gold and silver as these metals were to lead and copper. It was easy to manufacture and easy to handle. With ample money the paralysed industry and agriculture of France would start moving again. Money bore the same relation to industry as blood to the body, giving life and vigour to every part. Law advocated, in fact, what it was to take the world two hundred years to learn; that government spending which puts money into peoples' pockets is the quickest way to pull a sound country out of a depression and set it on the path to prosperity. "Wealth depends on commerce and commerce on circulation."

Law stated correctly the function of money. But he went further than this. He analysed the meaning of money. He pointed out that gold and silver was a commodity like everything else; that it fluctuated over the decades and therefore was not a constant factor. By using only gold and silver as money, France was not far removed from the primitive system of barter. Money should be employed on a far bigger scale. " What is needed," he said, " is credit." If a sound system of credit could be established the merchant with £100,000 could transact business on a scale of £1,000,000. Thus more men would be employed, more goods produced, more food grown, more wine sold. Although the Bank of England was in its infancy, Law emphasised the great benefits it had already conferred by the extension of credit. He declared that as a result England had as great an advantage over France in commerce as " a nation with firearms has over one with only bows and arrows."

Law's plan was to set up a state bank. The Council of Finance, however, refused to sanction this, but instead allowed him to found a private bank with himself as manager. This was established in his own house in the Place Vendôme, and gave Law the opportunity to prove his theories. Although he believed that eventually, when people had complete confidence in a paper currency based on government credit, gold and silver could be discontinued as a means of exchange, he realised the necessity of basing his currency on precious metals until that confidence was established. But how did he persuade people to accept paper money for their gold in the first place ? By the simple expedient of declaring that the paper would always be instantly redeemable; second, and more important, that it should always be redeemable in coin of a fixed weight and amount. For many years it had been the habit of the monarch to devalue coins whenever he felt like it; thus a gold coin worth £1 might overnight become worth only 15s. Now Mr. Law was guaranteeing paper money. If a bill was issued against a coin worth £1 it would be redeemable for £1 no matter whether or not the coin had dropped in value.

Law, of course, was gambling on his ability to persuade the Regent that altering coins was a bad practice.

Customers flocked to Law's bank. " The bills now furnished a currency safe and convenient in use, and of which the value could not be modified by any royal edict. They were sought for alike by citizens and by foreigners. If a contract was made payable in these bills, the parties could calculate with certainty on the liability assumed and the price to be received . . . Whenever presented for payment, they were promptly discharged *in specie*. The bank soon received the accounts of those who had money to deposit, and the demands of those who wished to borrow . . . The improvement in the financial condition that followed . . . attracted the attention of all. Merchants undertook new enterprises; manufacturers increased their products; the market for grain improved; the rate of interest fell."[1]

The Regent's patronage opened the doors of the most exclusive society in Paris. Mr. Law's manners were cool and perfect and he possessed remarkable tact in handling people. He made friends of the powerful Abbé Dubois and the Marquis d'Argenson who controlled the police and therefore controlled the internal affairs of the country. At the same time he did not neglect those who lacked power but possessed influence. For instance, he paid assiduous court to the Regent's mother who was always referred to as " Madame " and who spent most of her time writing letters. " Monsieur Law is very polite. I am greatly taken with him and he does all he can to please me," she confided to her half-sister. Saint-Simon was another whom Law courted. He went to see him every Tuesday morning to explain what he was doing, as a Cabinet minister might call on a monarch. Although the duke knew nothing about finance he could not help being flattered, and his acid pen softened when he mentioned the Scot. " He was a kind-hearted man, gentle and respectful in his manners."

Wherever the hawk-nosed financier went, he excited the

[1] *France under the Regency*: James Breck Perkins.

admiration of the ladies; yet he remained remarkably faithful to his strange, aloof wife who was his opposite in almost every way. Lady Catherine was dour and disdainful. She was thought to be truly English in her contempt for foreigners and her superior, ungracious manner. She despised French society and scarcely ever accompanied her husband to balls or parties. She was devoted to her children, a son and a daughter, and spent her time looking after them and running her house. Needless to say she was not a popular figure. " She came of a good English family," wrote Saint-Simon. " She had an ugly red blotch covering one eye and the upper part of her cheek, otherwise she was rather handsome; she was proud, overbearing, and very impertinent in her talk and manners, seldom returning any of the polite attentions offered to her; she paid few visits, but kept to her own house, where she exercised great authority. I do not know whether she had any influence over her husband in public affairs, but he always seemed to treat her with marked attention and respect."[1]

" My bank is not the only nor the greatest of my ideas," Law wrote to the Regent. " I will produce something which will surprise Europe by the changes which it will produce in favour of France—changes greater than have resulted from the introduction of credit . . . The regency of your highness, well employed, will suffice to increase the population to thirty millions, and the King's revenue to three hundred millions."

Law's idea was nothing short of State capitalism. He was the first propounder of a totalitarian economy. Although it was not based on " class warfare," it was very like the Soviet system of to-day. He believed that the State, or one huge company controlled by the State, and linked to the bank, should absorb all private industry. Private enterprise, he declared, was inefficient because small firms operated against each other in a higgledy piggledy fashion and inevitably cut each other's throats. A giant company with no rivals could be planned and controlled and act

---

[1] *Memoirs of the Duc de Saint-Simon*: Edited by Francis Arkwright, Stanley Paul & Co.

ruthlessly in the interest of the people as a whole. It could bring
to France incomparable wealth and make her the most powerful
country in the world.

Law was a marvellous talker. He was animated by such a
passionate belief in his theories he could almost be described as an
economic Messiah. He referred to his scheme as his " system,"
and soon fired the Regent with his own enthusiasm. The first
step in establishing his giant monopoly, he said, was to form a
company to develop the tracts in North America that the French
explorers Marquette and La Salle had claimed in the name of the
French King; that is, of course, if the Regent would rescind the
monopoly he had granted to a wealthy financier, by the name of
Crozat, and pass it on to Law.

The Regent assented. Crozat had not been able to do anything with his privileges as the capital required was beyond his
resources, and was only too thankful to retreat. In August, 1717,
Law's company, which came to be known as the Mississippi
Company, was created by royal letters patent. It was granted a
monopoly for twenty-five years of all commerce between France
and what was then known as the province of Louisiana. It was a
princely gift on a breathtaking scale, for it started at the mouth of
the Mississippi and stretched north for three thousand miles. It
included the present states of Louisiana, Mississippi, Arkansas,
Missouri, Illinois, Iowa, Wisconsin and Minnesota. Over this
vast area the Company could exercise the rights of a sovereign; it
could equip fleets, plant colonies, administer laws and raise armies.

Law's activities during the next two years must be divided into
two separate categories; one was the development of the
Mississippi Company as a business, the other the manipulation of
French finance. As far as the Mississippi Company went, Law lost
no time in promotion. He planned to raise 100,000,000 livres—
£5,000,000, a large sum for the times—by issuing shares to the
public at 500 livres each.[1] If he really had been able to lay his
hands on this huge sum and use it as he wished, the American

---

[1] The livre was roughly 20 to the £

continent might have become habitable years sooner. But Law
hit a snag. The Regent would only consent to the plan if
Mississippi stock were payable in the notes of the Government
which were then outstanding.[1] This meant that Law, instead of
being free to invest the capital of the Company in stores, forts and
warehouses, could only use the interest which at most would be
£200,000 a year.

This was not what Law desired, but he agreed to it. No doubt
he hoped to do a good deal of business on credit alone. He
ordered twenty ships to be built and launched an immense
publicity campaign to persuade volunteers to colonise the new
world. The territory he had been given was vast, but it was an
untamed wilderness inhabited by fierce savages. No Frenchman
could be much attracted by the life, but Law issued a spate of
pamphlets and prospectuses suggesting the fortunes that could
be made from furs and the discovery of precious metals. Law
believed implicitly in the natural wealth of this new continent;
first it was essential to get people to settle there, to build towns
and cities and make life safe, so that the great business of trade
with France could be carried out safely. He induced members of
the French nobility to organise their own groups of settlers.
He himself took a reservation in Arkansas and sent a party of
Germans to it. A French governor was appointed to Louisiana
and in 1717 laid the foundations of New Orleans, named in
honour of the Regent. Another group of settlers believed the
rumours, current at the time, that an enormous emerald rock
stood on the banks of the Arkansas river. Under the command of
a French officer they travelled seven hundred miles up the
Mississippi, but all they saw were huge prairies occupied by deer
and buffalo.

Volunteers were not plentiful and Law soon reverted to a
rather sinister method of collecting settlers. With the help of his

---

[1] i.e. the Government had given I.O.U.s for money it had borrowed from
the public. These I.O.U.s could be used to buy stock in the new
company.

friend, the Marquis d'Argenson, an edict was issued announcing that tramps, vagabonds and domestics out of employment for four days, would be sent off forcibly as colonists. As women were greatly in demand, prisons and hospitals were ransacked until a boatload of marriageable females were collected. The colonists were delighted when they arrived in Louisiana, and queued up to choose wives. Not all made suitable mates and the next boatload of women found far more reluctant suitors.

It was then decided to send married colonists. Law conceived the idea of releasing men and women from gaol so long as they would marry each other and set forth together. These weddings were staged flamboyantly to attract the widest attention. At St. Martin des Champs the wild ringing of bells summoned a curious crowd to watch one hundred and eight girls choosing husbands from a long line of prisoners. When they were all paired off, the priests married them. The couples were then transported to Paris where they were paraded through the streets. They were chained together, but historians are not clear as to whether this was a marriage symbol, or to prevent them from escaping.

Law's flair for publicity never flagged. He heard that a French officer had brought home with him a small party of Indians from Missouri. Among them was the daughter of the chief of the tribe. The group was invited to Paris and delighted the populace. Law arranged for them to perform Indian dances at the Italian theatre and to shoot stag in the Bois de Boulogne. They were endlessly fêted. The climax was reached when the chief's daughter agreed to be baptized in Notre Dame; and shortly afterwards announced that she would marry a French sergeant. Everyone was enchanted. The eight year old King of France sent gifts to the bride and the courtiers presented the warriors with blue coats trimmed with lace for the ceremony. Finally they all sailed back to Missouri and everyone confidently predicted that widespread conversions to the Roman Catholic faith would follow. But, alas, after some weeks, shocking news

Philippe, Duc d'Orleans, the dissolute Regent of France who presided over
the financial crisis in 1720

came back to France. The Indian bride had grown tired of her French husband and asked her chieftain father, as a favour, to massacre the French garrison and particularly her spouse. He had obliged.

The Regent backed Law enthusiastically but did not interfere. In many ways he was the perfect benefactor. He had complete faith in the Scot and gave him a free hand. The truth was that he was only too thankful to have someone shoulder the burden of France's finances. Philippe's nightly debauches were beginning to tell on him. The early hours of each morning found him dead drunk, and he was no longer able to get to his desk at eight. Besides, he was deeply worried by his daughter's health. His attachment to the nineteen year old Duchesse de Berri was so intense, he was often accused of incestuous relations with her. It was true that this strange, mad girl had such a hold on her father, she could do anything she liked. She was an odd mixture. By day she suffered from delusions of grandeur and by night she wallowed in the gutter. " Barring avarice," wrote St. Simon, " she suffered from every vice." She lived in the Palace of Luxembourg and kept 800 servants. She gave a ball so magnificent it took the court journal two months to describe it. Thirty-one soups and one hundred and thirty-one entremets were served; so much wine flowed that one hundred and thirty-two waiters were busy pouring it for twelve hours.

The Duchesse shocked the sticklers of court etiquette by insisting that guards surround her carriage, preceded by men sounding tymbals—an escort reserved for royalty. At the theatre she also demanded royal honours and when the public showed its disapproval, refused to attend any more. She would not heed any advice and even scoffed at the Church. When she was upbraided for not going to confession, she invited a Jesuit priest to live in her household, eat at her table and observe her debauches, so there would be nothing left to confess. However, she was superstitious. To be cured of an illness she made a vow that for six months her entourage would dress only in white. She treated Paris to the spectacle of an all-white carriage and harness with herself in virginal silks. At night the Duchesse shed her grandeur and consorted with anyone who amused her. She came under the spell of a low-born adventurer, named Riom, whom she secretly married.

The Duchesse de Berri's grandmother was appalled by her life. Most of all she was shocked by the amount of food the girl ate. " She is sick," wrote Madame, " because she has eaten enormously and drunk too much brandy." And again, " She cannot be well, she is such a glutton. Every night she sits down at the table at nine and eats until three in the morning."[1]

Madame predicted an early grave and she was right. In July, 1719, the twenty-four year old Duchesse died. The Regent sat by her bedside, weeping, for hours. " My son cannot sleep," wrote Madame. " The poor Duchesse de Berri could not be saved. Her head was full of water, she had an ulcer in her stomach and another in her thigh. The rest of her was like a pulp, and her liver was attacked. They took her secretly at night, followed by all her household, to St. Denis. Such difficulty did they have in composing her funeral oration that it was thought better to have none at all."[1]

While the Regent was occupied with his orgies and the sad fate of his daughter, John Law's financial schemes, on which he had been working for the past two years, began to come to fruition. Despite the publicity and the rumours of fabulous wealth in the new world, the shares of the Mississippi Company had not risen. Too many people had lost money on overseas investment to make the speculation seem worthwhile. In May, 1719, the stocks were selling at only 300 livres each, which was well below the par value of 500, or £25.

That month Law made a gesture which fired the public imagination. He announced that he had such confidence in the

[1] *Letters of Madame:* Ed. Scott Stevenson.

Mississippi Company, that he would make a bargain to buy 200 shares in six months' time at 500 livres each. " As a stock-jobbing operation it has few parallels in history," wrote one historian. " It was at once known that the manager of the Company of the West[1] was willing to take its stock six months in the future, at a price almost double that which it then commanded. If he made such a purchase, it must be because he knew of the gains that it was sure to realise, and of the further privileges with which the King proposed to endow it. The price of shares at once advanced, and the public began to seek for an investment that seemed destined to increase rapidly in value."[2]

The public was right. John Law did know of further gains and privileges. All the while that he had been promoting the Mississippi, he had been engaged in a series of transactions which would transform the Company into a giant octopus capable of embracing the whole structure of French trade and finance. This was essential in order to bring his " system "—State capitalism— into being. In 1718 he acquired the monopoly of the tobacco trade. In the spring and summer of 1719 he absorbed the East India Company, the China Company and the Africa Company, which gave him control of France's colonial trade. In July it was announced that he also had acquired the monopoly of the coinage; and in August the right to farm the taxes. Both these privileges meant a large yearly income.

Then came the sensation which marked the climax of Law's manipulations. He announced to a startled public that the Company was now ready to pay off the national debt which amounted to 1,500,000,000 livres, or £75,000,000. The scheme had been carefully thought out and this was how it worked. The Mississippi Company would give the Government 1,500,000,000 livres, which the Government, in turn, would repay to the

---

[1] The name of the Mississippi Company was changed first to the Company of the West, then to the Company of the Indies. We refer to it throughout as the Mississippi, since this was the name which clung and usually appears in contemporary letters and reports.

[2] *France under the Regency*: James Breck Perkins.

people from whom it had borrowed. It then would have only
one creditor, instead of thousands, and would pay the Mississippi
Company three per cent interest instead of the normal four per
cent. It is clear why the idea appealed to the Government, but
how could the Mississippi Company gain from it? The answer,
said Law, was simple. The people whose money was returned to
them would use it to buy shares in the Mississippi Company.
Thus the 1,500,000,000 would complete a circle. " The intention
of the Company," wrote Law, " is that the creditors shall invest
the money they receive in the shares which are now offered to
them at less than their value. Thus they will be enriched while
the State is relieved."

And that is exactly what the public did. Mississippi stock
first began to rise in May with Law's personal guarantee to buy
the shares at par in six months' time. With the announcement
that the Company had absorbed two other companies, new stocks
were issued, and these, too, began to rise. Indeed, in a month's
time they had doubled and were selling at 1,000 livres—£50.
In July, when the Company's right to the coinage was announced,
Law issued stock to pay the King for the concession, and the price
jumped to 2,000. This was followed by the right to farm the
taxes, and stocks were changing hands at 5,000. Lastly, came
Law's plan to pay off the national debt. More stocks were issued
to raise the necessary capital and the market price shot to 10,000,
then 13,000, then 15,000 and occasionally to 18,000 livres—or
£900.

The public frenzy was the most important factor in sending
up the value, but there were two other aspects that encouraged
the enthusiasm. The Regent had taken over Law's bank in 1718.
When it was run as a private concern, Law had insisted on keeping
a balance between gold reserves and paper currency; but now
he advised the Regent that sufficient confidence had been established in paper to forget gold entirely. The Government churned
out money like a printing press, and lent it at 1% and 2%. In the
spring of 1719 it issued £5,000,000 paper money; in June and

July another £15,000,000 and from July to Christmas a further
£40,000,000. The second factor that sent the market rocketing
was the right to buy shares on the instalment plan. A purchaser
could have his shares on the understanding that he would settle
for them in twelve monthly payments. This, of course, was what
we now call buying " on margin." With the markets rising every
day, and money easy to come by, it seemed a satisfactory way of
doing business.

There was no fear for the future, as " panics " and " depres-
sions " were unknown. There had never been a stock-market
" boom " before; indeed there had never been a stock market.
A small narrow street by the name of the rue Quincampoix had
been a resort for men dealing in government securities; it now
became the centre for the Mississippi speculation. There were no
brokers' offices and all the frenzied transactions took place in the
middle of the highway. The street was jammed with people and
traffic was barred. Gates were put up at either end. They were
opened at eight o'clock in the morning, drums were sounded and
the crowd poured in. From then until dark the street was a
bedlam of surging, shouting people, eager to buy and sell. The
owners of the houses along the Quincampoix did a thriving
business by renting their property to brokers at exorbitant fees.
A cobbler made thousands by putting chairs in the little shed and
having pen and ink ready for those who wished to write out
transactions; a hunchback was said to have done the same by
allowing people to use his hump as a desk.

The crowd was a fantastic mixture of priests, shop-keepers,
coachmen, servants and aristocrats, drawn from every part of
France. There was such a flood of people coming into Paris that
it was almost impossible to secure a seat on a coach except at an
exorbitant sum; besides this, foreigners from England, Holland
and Germany were arriving in droves. Some estimated a total
influx of three hundred thousand, and at some point or other they
all made their way to the rue Quincampoix. The lords and ladies
sat in the cafés sipping wine, playing quadrille and sending their

servants to execute their orders. This was nice for the servants who often made large profits. A valet was instructed to sell 250 shares for his master at 8,000. He found a purchaser at 10,000, kept the profit of 500,000 and began dealing in the shares himself. In a few weeks he was able to retire as a rich man.

This incident was not uncommon. As coachmen, waiters and bootblacks made fortunes, the word " millionaire " was coined and sprang into the European vocabulary. The common man had never dreamt that he could become rich. Now, with the possibility open to all, the masses were wild with joy. They looked upon the Scot as a master mind who had discovered the spring of eternal wealth. Law believed the same thing himself. When he appeared in the streets he was almost mobbed. Crowds surged around him trying to touch him and shouting " Long live Sieur Law! " He was delighted that the common people were bene-fiting from his financial revolution. When aristocrats exclaimed angrily that their cooks had become " millionaires," he reproved them for being old-fashioned, and wrote, " The gates of wealth are now open to all the world. It is that which distinguishes the fortunes of the old administration from those of the present."

The aristocrats, of course, did not suffer from neglect. Law believed it important to retain their good-will, and frequently reserved shares for important friends, which was tantamount to making them large gifts of money. One of the people he aided was the Duc de Bourbon who made over a million pounds, and spent it improving his palace at Chantilly, and importing 150 race horses at a time from England. Another was the Duc de la Force, but this gentleman did not fare so well. He had a passion for spices and porcelain, and imported them in such huge quantities that his jealous fellow-aristocrats declared he had be-come a merchant and must forfeit his right to a peerage. Among the English visitors who benefited was Lord Belhaven, a gentle-man of the bedchamber to the Prince of Wales; he was rumoured to be buying for his royal master and was said to have taken a handsome profit home with him. Another was Joseph Gage, the brother of the first Viscount Gage. He profited so prodigiously "that he offered three million sterling to Augustus, King of Poland, to resign that crown in his favour; and on the refusal of that monarch to accede to these terms, entered into a negotiation for the purchase of the sovereignty of the island of Sardinia; but the treaty did not take effect." The Polish crown had been sold before, but three millions was considered a grudging sum; this inspired Mr. Pope to write:

The Crown of Poland, venal twice an age
To just three millions stinted modest Gage.

Indeed, the powerful personages who did not speculate in Mississippi stock were so rare they deserve special mention. The Duc de Saint-Simon refused to become involved, despite the fact that he was a close friend of Law, and continually pressed to accept shares. He insisted that he knew nothing of finance and was well content with his present lot in life. Another striking example was the Earl of Stair. He liked to gamble and was always hard-pressed for funds, yet he felt it would set a bad example for a British Ambassador to withdraw money from England to buy French stocks. "I have been in the wrong to myself to the value of thirty or forty thousand pounds," he wrote to Mr. Craggs, one of the Secretaries of State in London, "which I might very easily have gained if I had put myself, as others did, into Mr. Law's hands; but I thought it my duty, considering my station, not to do so."[1]

Stories of Law's kindnesses in securing shares for friends spread like wild-fire and he was pursued shamelessly. People stopped at nothing to make his acquaintance. One lady gave orders to her coachman to arrange an accident when she approached Mr. Law. The lady spotted her victim first, and was heard to shout imperiously, "Now you rascal! Overturn the carriage! Now!" Apparently the coachman did as he was bid, and Mr. Law came to her rescue, but no one knows whether she

[1] *Annals of Viscount Stair.*

managed to wheedle any shares from him. Another lady had an
unfortunate slip of the tongue. When she met Law she meant to
say, " *Faites-moi un concession.*" She was so excited she said
instead, " *Faites-moi un conception.*" " You come too late,"
Law replied dryly. " It is no longer possible for me."

Law held morning levees which were crowded with " Princes,
Dukes and Peers, Marshals and Prelates, who all humbled themselves before his shrine with the utmost submission." The Regent
and his mother, Madame, had both made a great deal of money
from the boom, and could look upon the scene with contented
detachment. Madame was particularly amused by the way the
members of her own sex behaved. " Law is so run after that he
has no rest day and night," she wrote. " A Duchess kissed his
hands before everyone, and if Duchesses kiss his hands, what part
of him won't the other ladies salute ?"

III

THE SOUTH SEA SCHEME

Across the channel, the gentlemen who governed for George I followed John Law's activities with deep attention. Lord Stair the British ambassador to Paris, sent agitated dispatches to London. "You must henceforth look upon Law as the first minister," he wrote on September 1st, 1719, "whose daily discourse is, that he will raise France to a greater height than ever she was, upon the ruin of England . . ." The astonishing news that a Briton was virtually Prime Minister of France was received with a mixture of pride and apprehension. Was Stair right? Was Law really plotting Britain's downfall?

The minister in charge of foreign affairs, Earl Stanhope, found Lord Stair's assertions hard to believe. He had been aware of Law, both as a power and a personality, ever since 1716 when the latter had pulled off a remarkable coup by persuading the Regent of France to buy the fabulous Pitt diamond . . . "as big as a great egg." This diamond was the property of Mr. Thomas Pitt (grandfather of the future Earl of Chatham), a hot-tempered, merchant adventurer who had been appointed Governor of Madras in 1698. The reason Lord Stanhope had followed the negotiations so closely was because Pitt was his father-in-law, and the old man had driven the family nearly crazy with his talk about the diamond. He had bought the stone in 1701 from an Indian dealer by the name of Jamachund. It had come out of the Golconda mines and was the biggest diamond ever seen. It weighed 410 carats in the rough and 135 when cut as a brilliant. Pitt decided to risk everything and buy it as a speculation. If he could find the right purchaser for it, he could lay the foundation

73

of a family fortune. For three months he haggled over the price. Finally he agreed to pay the huge sum of £25,000. His decision took great courage for he was not a rich man. He sent his son, Robert back to Europe with the stone, to start at once to look for a buyer. Poor Robert had a wretched time. The old man pursued him by every post with strictures about his " great concerne." " You will see that I have wrote in my joint letter, that the chest shall stand in the Bank of England. That of blowing open or carrying away the chest may be done, but I hope my sons would not let the actors of it survive such a villainy. And I wish in showing of it (which I would have you withstand without good reasons there be for it) you see there is no trick played to slide it away and put a christiall in the room of the same magnituce. I charge you that you never take the stone out upon any occasion but that you your self weigh it when you take it out and when you put it in, and that it never be out of your eye as much as in shifting one hand to another."[1]

Robert had a model made of the stone and hawked it to almost every court in Europe; but it was always refused because the price was too high. Pitt was furious at each rejection. " I will not part with it under £1500 a carat, which I am sure is as cheap as Nick-beef, and let any Potentate buy it, the next day 'tis worth a million pounds of sterling."

Pitt returned to Europe in 1710 and for five years tried vainly to dispose of it himself. Then he heard of John Law and his newly founded bank in Paris. He sent the model to him and asked if he would try and interest the Regent in it. Law enjoyed doing favours but this was no easy task in view of France's impoverished state. Pitt had little hope of a deal. Law's success came as a complete surprise. From that moment Lord Stanhope took notice of the Scot as a power to be reckoned with. St. Simon describes the negotiations in his memoirs, and they throw a light on Law's shrewdness in handling people. " A man employed in the Great Mogul's diamond mines contrived to secret a very large

---

[1] *England Under Queen Anne*: G. M. Trevelyan.

stone, which he carried off to Europe.[1] He showed it to several Princes, and finally took it to England, where the King admired it, but could not make up his mind to buy it. A model of it was made in crystal, and sent to Law, who suggested to the Regent that he should buy it for the King. The Regent, however, was startled by the price demanded and refused. Law, who in many things had a very noble way of thinking, came to me with the model. I agreed with him that it was unworthy of the greatness of a King of France to allow himself to be deterred by a question of money when he had the chance of acquiring an inestimable and unique jewel; and the fact that it had been refused by other sovereigns ought to make us more determined not to let the opportunity slip. Law was delighted to hear me express these sentiments, and begged me to speak to the Regent.

" The state of the finances was the Duke of Orléans' principal objection; he was afraid of being blamed if he made such a costly purchase at a time when it was difficult to meet the most necessary payments, and everybody was suffering. I said these considerations no doubt had great weight; still he ought not to look on the affairs of the greatest King in Europe quite in the same light as those of a private person. It would be very reprehensible for a private person to throw away 100,000 livres on a diamond at a time when he was deeply in debt; but in this case he must think of the honour of the Crown, and not lose this chance of acquiring a priceless diamond, far finer than any in Europe; the purchase would confer lasting honour on his Regency; and, after all, the finances were in so bad a condition that the relief to be obtained by refraining from it would be almost imperceptible. I did not leave him till I had prevailed on him to buy the diamond.

" In the meanwhile Law had impressed on the vendor the great difficulty he would have in disposing of such a jewel, and in this way contrived to beat down the price, which was finally fixed at 2,000,000 livres,[2] besides the fragments resulting from the

[1] This, of course, was not the true version.
[2] The price paid in sterling was £133,000.

cutting. [The vendor] was to receive the interest of the purchase money, and took away jewels to the value of 2,000,000 livres in pledge till we could pay the principal. The Duke of Orléans was agreeably surprised to find that the public expressed great satisfaction with the purchase. The diamond was called 'The Regent'; it is about the size of a greengage plum, of the purest water, perfectly white, and without a flaw of any sort."[1]

When Lord Stair, the ambassador, was in England on leave in December, 1716, Lord Stanhope impressed him with John Law's importance and instructed him to try and strike up a close friendship with the Scot. Stair assented, but he was not a happy choice as a diplomat. He was a clever man, tall and handsome, with a record of gallantry for his services in Marlborough's army. But his personality was unfortunate; his manner was so arrogant, he antagonised nearly everyone he met. "He carried his head high, with a most insolent expression," wrote Saint-Simon. "He tried to mingle with the best society, which soon became tired of his impertinent talk, though he did his best to attract people to his house by keeping an excellent cook."

There is no doubt that Stair believed implicitly in the superiority of the British. His keenness to outstrip the French, even in social events, bordered on the ridiculous. When he made his "formal entry" into Paris he spent thousands of pounds on carriages and livery, and everyone was forced to admit it was the grandest procession of its kind ever seen. Nevertheless it irritated the French, and the Regent delighted the aristocracy by the counter-action he took. When Stair drove up to the Tuileries in a carriage drawn by eight horses, to wait upon the King and the Regent, he was informed by the master of ceremonies that only carriages with two horses could enter the *cour du roi*. He had no alternative but to withdraw six horses and drive to the palace with a pair.

Stair could not bear to think that any Frenchman could live

[1] *Memoirs of the Duc de Saint-Simon*: Ed. Francis Arkwright, Stanley Paul & Co.

in greater style than a British ambassador. Consequently he ran
up huge expenses. In order to meet his debts, he took to gambling
and the debts soared even higher. He received many sharp re-
proaches from London, particularly from his friend, James Craggs,
who shared the duties of Secretary of State with Lord Stanhope.
" Your expenses are exorbitant and I do not see how they will be
made up to you," wrote Craggs in October, 1718, " I am upon
this occasion going to say a disagreeable thing, which is, that you
cannot imagine what prejudice your play does you with everybody, and how much it enervates the attempts of your friends to
serve you . . . God knows, I desire nothing hardly more than to
be serviceable to you; and your qualifications and services might
carry you where you pleased, were it not for that damnable
witchcraft . . ."[1]

Somehow the Earl of Stair managed to keep his head above
water. He did as Stanhope bid him and kept in close touch with
John Law. However in the autumn of 1719, as Law was moving
from strength to strength, Stair had a violent quarrel with him
which made a permanent breach. They met at a friend's house
and apparently Stair lost his temper when he heard Law boasting
that he would make France the first power in Europe at the
expense of England. Stair flew into a rage, told Law that he was
nothing but a mountebank and more likely to ruin France with
his crazy schemes than enhance her power.

This is what Stair truly believed, as many of his letters show.
But what is interesting is the fact that once he had had his quarrel,
he began to take Law with deadly seriousness. There is no more
talk about Law's system being doomed to failure. From then on
he sent urgent dispatches to London echoing Law's own assertions; that France might dominate Europe on the ruin of
England's economic structure. His mind raced forward; he saw
Law becoming so much the master that he might attempt putting
a Stuart on the English throne; and the climax could mean war
between the two countries. " My dear Craggs, take my word for

[1] *Annals of Viscount Stair.*

it Mr. Law's plan is formed to destroy the King and his government, and our nation, and he will certainly bring his master into
it . . . There is nothing but an appearance of strength or firmness
on our side, or the miscarriage of Law's system on this side, that
can save us from a war with France . . ."[1]

Then Stair did an extraordinary thing; without any instructions from London he went to the Regent and warned him that
Law was causing a breach between England and France. "I
represented to the Duke of Orléans that Law, by his vanity and
presumption, was leading him into great dangers and incon-
veniences both at home and abroad; that Law, by going too fast,
and by taking arbitrary measures, was in a way to ruin his Highness's credit with the nation, and to overturn the whole system of
the finances; and that, at the same time, Law was, by his discourse and his conduct, doing everything that lay in his power to
destroy the good understanding between the King and the
Regent and between the Regent and the rest of his allies; and I
bade the Regent beware how he trusted the reins of his chariot
to that Phaeton Law, because he would overturn it." [1]

Stair had his interview with the Regent in December, a few
weeks after his quarrel. Law was just approaching the summit of
his power. The Regent wanted to make him Prime Minister,
de jure as well as *de facto*. This was not possible since the Scot
was not a Catholic. However rumours spread that Law was to be
converted, and proved to be correct. He accepted the Roman
Catholic faith and during the first week of January, 1720, was
made Comptroller General of France's finances, the highest
political office in the land. He was the most famous minister in
Europe. His native city of Edinburgh, proud of having produced
such a great figure, sent him the freedom of the city in a gold box
worth £300.

Mr. Secretary Craggs was dismayed by Lord Stair's quarrel
with Law. He was a genuine well-wisher and wrote plaintively,
"If your lordship asks my opinion, I could really wish that after

---

[1] *Annals of Viscount Stair.*

having so often told us we must henceforth look upon Law as first minister, you had not openly attacked him . . ." Lord Stanhope, on the other hand, was not nearly so polite. He was in a towering rage. He was furious at Stair, first for the quarrel, second for complaining to the Regent about Law. The fellow was quite impossible, he must be recalled. Stanhope decided there was nothing to do but to make a trip to Paris himself, and try and re-establish good relations with Law. He arrived in the French capital a day or so before Law's appointment as Comptroller General. He did not stay with Lord Stair as it was impossible for the ambassador to invite the new Prime Minister to the Embassy. He saw both Law and the Regent and threw Lord Stair to the wolves. He apologised deeply for the views his ambassador had expressed and emphasised that they were completely un-authorised. He was so displeased, he said, that he was going to appoint a new envoy. What was extraordinary was that he did not bother to acquaint Stair with this news. He let him learn about it through gossip.

Stair had reason to be hurt and angry. He wrote to Mr. Craggs, " Since Lord Stanhope has thought fit to intimate my recall to the ministers of this court, who have taken care to publish it through all the town, I hope that the King will send as soon as possible some confidential person to Paris, where, unless I am much mistaken, His Majesty will soon require an enlightened minister."[1] He went on to criticise Stanhope for not staying at the Embassy and for the policy of appeasement he was adopting. He believed strong words would bring better results.

Poor wobbly Mr. Craggs liked to please the great men around him. But he had no option but to write the Earl of Stair a blunt letter. The King had ordered Stanhope to talk with Law, and judge the situation as well as he could. " Your Lordship had put things upon that foot with this man, or he with you, that 'twas not possible for him to set foot within your house. Was Lord Stanhope, who was dispatched to see whether Hannibal was at

[1] *Annals of Viscount Stair.*

the gates, to be disputing punctilios . . . either not to have gone to your house that he might receive the first visit from Mr. Law, or when he was there, pass that fortnight he stayed in a negotiation to meet with a man the King had absolutely directed him to talk with? . . . I will agree entirely to one thing with you that Law may so settle and establish the finances of France as to make that kingdom more formidable than ever to its neighbours. I think we ought to tremble at it, and be very cautious and look well about us. I do agree that he may have the vanity, being our country-man, some time or other to *attempt giving us a monarch*; and this must make us very watchful, but I can never consent that the King should, because of these apprehensions, immediately break with the Regent unless he will remove Mr. Law . . . If that is your mind I differ with you entirely. Would you have us then continue in every thing to oppose and irritate Mr. Law? I remember you being very near with the Abbé Dubois as you have since been with Law. You are now going I see to fall out at home with Lord Stanhope, and pray what is to come of all this? I vow to God you put me in mind of what I have so often seen you do at play, that when you began to lose, you would, though it was against all the sharpers and swordsmen in the Den, play on for all you was worth."[1]

Lord Stanhope and his colleagues were not the only English-men concerning themselves with Mr. Law. The business world in general, and Mr. John Blunt in particular, had been following the Scotsman's progress with fascinated attention. Blunt was a short, plump, unscrupulous little man who loved the feel and manipulation of money. His whole being was dedicated to its acquisition. He was the son of a Rochester shoemaker and had started life as a " petty scrivener in Birchin Lane, where part of his business was to write letters for a groat or a sixpence." He saved money at great sacrifice, and made more by lending it out at high rates. Eventually he was able to set up as a merchant but

[1] *Annals of Viscount Stair.*

his real interest centred on company promoting. He was not an attractive personality; when he was not working on some sharp deal he was quoting the Bible and inveighing against vice. He launched two companies, one to do with linen, the other bringing water to London. The shareholders lost heavily but Blunt acquired a small fortune. Now he was a figure in the City. He was elected to the Common Council for the Ward of Cornhill, and in 1711 was appointed one of the first directors of the South Sea Company. His vitality and passion for gain soon made him the dominant figure on the board.

Blunt followed Mr. John Law's activities with riveted attention. He was certain that Law's decision to take over the French national debt had been prompted by the example of the South Sea Company, which, as the reader will recall, had incorporated ten million pounds of Government debt into its stock when it was founded. The Government paid yearly interest of 5%; and since the Company's trade with the Spanish colonies in South America had never fully materialised, this provided its main source of revenue.

The war with Spain in 1718 suspended all attempts to trade. Early in 1719, largely for want of anything better to do, the Company conceived the idea of again taking over Government debt, this time the lottery loan. A million and a half pounds had been borrowed by the State at a high rate of interest. The South Sea Company would lower the rate, and try to entice the public into exchanging their securities for South Sea stock in the hope of a future expansion of trade. The plan had worked well; and the South Sea Company had made a capital gain of over seventy thousand pounds, which represented the difference between the par value of its stock and the market price, when the conversion took place.

Blunt was convinced that Mr. Law had drawn his inspiration from these examples of a private trading-company's incursion into the world of finance. Now it was his turn to draw inspiration from Mr. Law. Although Law's scheme of absorbing all the

trading companies in France into one giant co-operation was far
more grandiose, Blunt believed that the South Sea Company
could go him one better. What if the South Sea took over the
whole of the British national debt? The sum amounted to fifty
million pounds; thirty million had been borrowed from the
public at large; and twenty million from the East India Company
and the Bank of England. If Blunt's project was accepted the
South Sea Company would dominate the Far Eastern trade, and
the Bank would be its hand-maiden.

But this was not all. Blunt saw a chance of millions of pounds
of profit, not only for the Company, but for private individuals
as well. This was the idea. The par value of South Sea stock was
£100 a share. If Parliament agreed to the taking over of the
national debt it would authorise the Company to strike £100
of new stock for every £100 of debt it converted. At the
moment, the market value of South Sea shares was £128. But
suppose that the market price rose to £300. If an individual
holding £1,200 of Government securities wanted to convert
them into South Sea stock, the Company would be allowed to
issue 12 new shares at £100 each. But it would only have to
give the creditor four of those shares if the market price was
£300. It would then have 8 surplus shares for sale, which would
bring it a profit of £2,400. Of course everything depended on
raising the price of the stock. But Blunt had studied Mr. Law's
publicity methods and he was sure it could be done.

Mr. Blunt's co-directors were staggered and excited by his
idea. They had never thought on such a huge scale. He did not
stress his private plans for raising the price of the stock, but carefully explained how the transaction could be beneficial both to
the Government and the Company. The directors knew they
were on a good thing, for both Parliament and the business
world were obsessed by the national debt. Every speech and
every newspaper referred to the " heavy burden " under which
the nation was labouring. Until William's reign and the long
wars against Louis XIV, Britain had balanced its budget year by

year; now the debt had become enormous, and the fact that no one knew how to get rid of it, was likened to a permanent mill-stone around a swimmer's neck.

Blunt was authorised to put the scheme to the Government. He realised that it would need expert handling, and scrutinised the political situation carefully. The two Earls—Sunderland and Stanhope—dominated the Government, but neither understood or liked " finance." They regarded such matters as " middle-class," and had as little to do with them as possible. Although Sunderland was First Lord of the Treasury, he had succeeded in getting a mediocre servile man named Mr. Aislabie appointed as Chancellor of the Exchequer. Aislabie relieved Sunderland of the work, and remained obediently in the background.

Blunt decided to approach Stanhope. The latter received him and apparently read his proposal, but returned it saying that he was not competent to offer an opinion on financial affairs. Blunt then tried Sunderland, but the noble earl considered himself too grand to be bothered with " a tradesman " and referred him to the Chancellor of the Exchequer. Blunt fumed at the slight, but had no alternative save to do as he was told.

He unfolded his plan to Mr. Aislabie who was startled by the magnitude of it. Aislabie was not a clever man, but he could see at once that the idea of taking over the debts owed by the Government both to the East India Company and the Bank of England would arouse a fury of opposition from the two concerns, and be fought tooth and nail. After all, the Bank was the darling of the Whig Party and the East India Company the pride of the Whig business man. They would not tamely consent to become subsidiaries of the South Sea Company. Blunt saw the sense of Aislabie's argument. Working in conjunction with his close friend, Robert Knight, the Company treasurer, and Mr. Grigsby, a distant relation and the Company accountant, he drew up a new plan. He went back to Aislabie, and this time proposed that the South Sea Company should convert only the thirty million pounds which the Government owed to the general public. The

Chancellor approved the scheme and the ball started rolling. The first hint came in the King's speech delivered in November, 1719. " I must desire you to turn your thoughts to all proper means of lessening the debts of the nation."

In the meantime John Blunt had not been idle. The South Sea directors had appointed a sub-committee to do everything in its power to get the Bill accepted by Parliament. This committee consisted of Blunt and Knight, Sir John Fellows, the Sub-Governor, Charles Joye, the Deputy-Governor, Edward Gibbon (grandfather of the historian), Richard Houlditch and Robert Chester.

The committee discussed the problems facing it. Even with the revised plan, Blunt knew that the Bank of England, from a prestige point of view alone, would oppose them with all its force. It could not stand idly by and allow a trading concern to take its place as the chief finance house of the nation. Besides, the old enmity between the two companies still smouldered. The Bank was a Whig creation, whereas the South Sea Company had been brought into the world and nurtured by the Tories. Strong sentiments would be aroused, and the Bill was bound to have a stormy passage. Furthermore there would be the formidable opposition of Robert Walpole. Walpole was an ex-Chancellor of the Exchequer; a strong supporter of the Bank; and a pungent speaker. For nearly three years he had been out of the Government and would not hesitate to attack. Indeed, as the Committee debated their problems he gave an unexpected exhibition of his strength. Almost single-handed he slew the Government's Peerage Bill, much to the annoyance of the Earl of Sunderland. But perhaps this was a good sign from the South Sea point of view. It was known that both he and Lord Townshend were looking for a way back to office; Walpole might not deem it prudent to continue making himself a nuisance.

Nevertheless, the Committee decided not to run any risks. They would counter the opposition by promising " rewards " for unwavering support. Blunt consulted Aislabie, who had already been appraised of the advantages that might come his way, and Aislabie suggested a talk with Mr. James Craggs, the Postmaster-General, father of the Mr. Craggs who was joint secretary at the Foreign Office. Craggs the elder was a hard-headed, self-made business man who had originally come from Durham, and who often served as a go-between. He had begun his career in this capacity, when he secured a job as footman to the Duchess of Norfolk. He spent most of his time taking messages to her lovers. He received large tips in return for his discretion and finally was able to set himself up as an Army Clothes Contractor. He was not hampered by scruples and made huge profits. These did not pass unnoticed, and he was accused of dishonesty and sent to the Tower. The Duke of Marlborough felt sorry for him and gave him a job as manager of his private affairs. Craggs' passion in life was his son, whom he named after himself and who usually was referred to as " Craggs the younger." He gave the boy every advantage and was thrilled to see him become a gentleman of fashion with entrée into the most exclusive circles of the day. Craggs the elder handled Marlborough's affairs brilliantly, and when George I came to the throne the Duke repaid him by urging the King to give him and his son places in the Government.

Craggs the elder brought Craggs the younger into the South Sea adventure, after being assured that both would find it a beneficial undertaking. The Foreign Office Craggs gave sound advice. First of all the King's favourites must be bought, and knowing the prices they usually commanded for favours, £10,000 each was the lowest sum that would be acceptable. Also it might be wise to make a small gift to Madame Kielmansegge's nieces.

Then there was the Earl of Sunderland. Craggs did not think he would look askance at a gift; at any rate there was no harm in trying him. The Earl Stanhope, on the other hand, was a different kettle of fish. His incorruptibility had become almost a by-word, and was regarded by many as straight priggishness. Only recently the French Foreign Secretary, the Abbé Dubois, had offered Stanhope £40,000 for his signature on a treaty. Although Stanhope signed, he refused to take a penny, and the Abbé wrote sadly to the Regent. " It is the only thing in the negotiations in which I have entirely failed."

Luckily Earl Stanhope had a young cousin, Mr. Charles Stanhope, who looked upon life in a more worldly way. He had the same excellent contacts as his kinsman and was Secretary to the Treasury as well. Last, but equally important, came the Members of Parliament. At least a hundred of these gentlemen would have to be approached and offered inducements. Blunt and Craggs apportioned the task between them and set to work.

At last the stage was ready. Mr. Aislabie introduced the South Sea proposals to the House of Commons on January 22nd. This is how he put it. If Parliament allowed the South Sea Company to convert £30,000,000 of national debt, the following advantages would be gained by the Government. First, the Government would be granted a 1% reduction in the rate of interest it was paying (from 5% to 4%) after 1727. This 1% saving would amount to about £300,000 a year. Furthermore the Company would pay a large capital sum for the privilege of undertaking the conversion. This would mean another saving of interest of roughly £150,000 per annum. If the Government put its savings aside every year, the Chancellor explained, the whole national debt could be wiped out in twenty-five years. He emphasised that as far as the public was concerned the scheme was purely voluntary. No government creditor would be forced to convert his holdings for South Sea stock unless he felt the bargain worth it. When he had finished, Secretary Craggs congratulated him on his convincing arguments, then sat down and waited for comment.

The House sat dumbfounded. It was a stupendous idea, but difficult to grasp. The gain to the Government was obvious; but how w ould the creditors profit, or even the South Sea Company for that matter ? And why was the Bank of England not handling the conversion? "A profound silence ensued for a full quarter of an hour"; wrote Thomas Brodrick, M.P., to his brother, the Lord Chancellor of Ireland, "everyone expecting who would first rise; when the Secretary getting up to make his motion in form, I rose, and was pointed to. I readily agreed with the two gentlemen who had spoake, that till the nationall debt was discharged, or att least in a fair way of being soe, we were not to expect making that figure we formerly had. I sayd, I could goe farther, making use of the expression of a gentleman (Mr. Hutchyson) whoe told us in a former session, that till this was done, wee could not (properly speaking) call ourselves a nation; that therefore every scheme or proposal tending thereto, ought to be received and considered ... The occasion of my now speaking was, that the first gentleman who spoake, seemed to mee to recommend the scheme nott onely in opposition, but even exclusively of all others; and that the next had chimed in with him; that I hoped, in order to make the best bargaine wee could, every other company, nay any other society of men might bee att as full liberty to make proposals as the South Sea Company, since every gentleman must agree, this to be the likelyest way to make a good bargain for the publique.

" Our great men lookt as if thunderstruck, and one of them in particular, turned as pale as my cravate. Uppon this ensued a debate of above two hours. Our ministers (as they might in a committee) spoake again and again; for their auxiliarys proved faint hearted. Mr. Aislaby, in heat, used this unguarded expression; Things of this nature must bee carried on with a *spiritt*; to which Sir Joseph Jekill, with a good deal of warmth, tooke very just exception; this *spiritt*, sayes hee, is what has undone the nation; our businesse is to consider thoroughly, deliberate calmly, and judge of the whole uppon reason, nott with the *spiritt* mentioned. Mr. Aislaby desired to explaine; sayd hee only meant that creditt was to bee soe supported; which caused some smiling. Mr. Walpole applauded the designe, and agreed in general to the reasonablenesse of the scheme, wherein however something wanted amendment, and others (although but few) were unreasonable; but concluded strongly for hearing all, as indeed every body did, three or four onely excepted. Mr. Lechmere answer'd him but little, God worr, to the matter in hand; for quitting that, he fell into invectives against Walpole's former scheme, giving great preferences to this. The town says, the bargaine with the South Sea Company was agreed att his chambers, between Mr. Aislaby, Sir George Caswell, and three or four other South Sea-men; since which, they say Mr. Aislaby has bought £27,000 stock."[1]

Mr. Aislabie had hoped to rush the South Sea bill through before the opposition had time to gather its wits; but the Bank's supporters had been too quick for him. They insisted that " if an advantage was to be made by publick bargains, the Bank should be preferr'd before a Company that has never done anything for the Nation . . ." And the debate closed with the agreement that the Bank should be allowed time to put forward proposals of its own.

The battle was on. A few days later the Bank made an offer; the South Sea Company made a second offer; the Bank came back with still a further offer. These were the two schemes in their final forms. The Bank would pay the Government £5,600,000 for the privilege of carrying out the conversion; it would reduce the interest payable by the Government from 5% to 4% in 1724; and lastly, " that no Doubt may remain of their sincere Intentions," they would offer the holders of long annuities £1700 Bank stock for every hundred pounds per annum which they (the annuitants) were now receiving.

The South Sea Company, on the other hand, offered the Government £7,500,000 for the right to convert the debt; it also agreed to reduce the Government's interest in 1724; but instead of stating clearly, as the Bank had, how much capital stock it would give to the annuitants, it merely said that if annuitants were not satisfied with the offer made to them and

[1] *The Political State of Great Britain.*

refused to convert, it would pay a fine of over £600,000 to the Government. Mr. Aislabie later declared that he was appalled when he was told that the South Sea Company was going to bid as high as £7,500,000 for permission to put its scheme into operation. He suggested to Blunt sharing the conversion with the Bank, but the little man replied indignantly, " No, sir! we will never divide the child."

Robert Walpole spoke in favour of the Bank, as Aislabie had foreseen; but the fact that the South Sea Company was willing to pay a premium, almost two million higher than the Bank for the conversion privilege, carried the day for it. No one knows the words or even the arguments that were used, as no records have been preserved. However the spate of pamphlets that were published a few weeks later reveals what people were thinking. The Bank supporters and business men saw clearly the way in which the South Sea Company intended to make its profit. The £30,000,000 to be converted consisted of £15,000,000 of redeemable debts and £15,000,000 irredeemable debts, or annuities.[1] According to the critics everything centred on the annuities. Let's take a look at it. If you were receiving an annuity of £100 a year, classed as "irredeemable," what would you declare the purchase price to be worth? The Government had fixed the value at £2,000 (or in financial language, at 20 years' purchase) for the purpose of transferring the debt. Since you were not obliged to exchange your Government securities for stock in a private company, what would you have considered a fair offer? The Bank had promised you 17 shares of Bank stock at par value of £100 a share. Since Bank stock was selling in the market at £150 a share this was the equivalent of £2,500. The South Sea Company, on the other hand, had not stated what it

---

[1] The redeemable debts were loans which had to be repaid whether on demand or at stated intervals; the annuities, on the other hand, might be likened to pensions, purchased for a lump sum which was not returnable. The people who invested their money in annuities were those who wished to secure themselves or their children a safe, permanent income.

would offer. The critics said they knew why. The Company would see how high it could drive the price of its stock, by converting the redeemable debts first. If stock could be raised to £300 a share the directors would not have to give you 17 shares of capital stock, as the Bank had proposed to do, but only 9 shares, which would be worth £2,700. And the directors would have 11 surplus shares which they could sell to the public, taking in a profit of £3,300. " Now it must be obvious to everyone, that it can never be to the [South Sea] Company's interest to bring in the Annuitants, before all the redeemable funds are paid off, and the new stock is struck and sold; for that would be to call in sharers to divide the great sum with themselves and lessen their profits by half . . ."[1]

The critics of the South Sea Company fought hard. The Government had such a large majority they could not prevent the Company converting the debt; but at least they could diminish its opportunity for speculation by forcing the directors to declare what capital stock they would give to the annuitants. This, then, was the spanner they tried to throw into the works. The opposition members of Parliament, led by Robert Walpole, framed a motion and canvassed members to gain support. In the meantime the pamphleteers were not idle. One writer declared that if the South Sea Directors refused so reasonable a request they would reveal themselves as men " who design not the public interest but their own . . . who have been cooking up a project for seven or eight months past, under the Pretense of paying off the publick debts, but in truth to new-burthen the publick and enrich themselves; and who if they are let alone, will turn this great design into a private job; and when they have work'd up their stock by management to an unnatural price, will draw out and leave the publick to shift for itself, until the season comes around again for gathering new plumbs." [2]

A supporter of the South Sea Company answered the argu-

[1] *A Comparison between the Proposal of the Bank and the South Sea Company.*
[2] *The Political State of Great Britain.*

ment with the incredibly naïve assertion that " if the House of Commons should ever really come to a Resolution of obliging them [the South Sea Company] to declare how much stock they would give the Annuitants, the Price of their Stock must certainly fall very greatly By which not one individual Annuitant would subscribe, and the Nation be still left to struggle faintly under this oppressive Burthen."[1]

Robert Walpole's motion was introduced to the House on March 23rd. Aislabie and Blunt, despite all the precautions they had taken were nervous. They could tell from the talk in the coffee houses that the pamphleteers were having considerable effect; and Aislabie knew by the temper of the House that it was bound to be a close fight. The motion begged the House " to receive proposals from the South Sea Company, whereby it might be fix'd and determin'd what Share or Shares of and in the to be increased Capital stock of the Said Company, the proprietors of the said annuities should be entitled to have and enjoy..." This motion " occasion'd a very warm debate, that lasted from one of the clock in the afternoon, till near seven in the evening, in which Robert and Horatio Walpole, Esquires, Mr. Pitt, Mr. Gould, Sir Richard Steele, and some other gentlemen spoke in favour of the Annuitants..."

The South Sea Company supporters, with their huge majority refused to be ruffled. They replied " that the obliging the South Sea Company to fix a Price upon the Annuities, might endanger the Success of so beneficial an Undertaking: That as it was the Interest of the Company to take in the said Annuities, so no Doubt was to be made, but they would use all their Endeavours for that Purpose; and would offer such advantageous Conditions to the Annuitants, as would encourage them to come in voluntarily. That therefore they ought to allow the said Company a competent Time to try what they could do; and if in a subsequent session of Parliament it should appear, that the Conditions they had offer'd to the Annuitants were not reasonable, and con-

[1] *An Argument.*

sequently had proved ineffectual, the Commons, in such a Case, might give what Directions they should think proper about the Matter. These, and other Reasons, that were urged on the same Side, had so much weight, that the Question being put upon the Motion before-mentioned, it passed in the Negative, by a Majority of 144 Voices against 140."[1]

The Government had squeaked home by only four votes; but this was enough. The unknown Parliamentary reporter who handed down the scene to posterity goes on to say, " It is to be observ'd that whilst this great Affair was debating in the House of Commons, the Stock-Jobbers in Exchange Alley, were in perpetual Hurry, being toss'd about between Hopes and Fears, upon the different Accounts they receiv'd, almost every Minute, from their Agents and friends in Westminster: But as soon as it was known, That the Clause offer'd to cramp the South-Sea Company's Project had been rejected, the Stocks of that Company, which, since the Commons had accepted their scheme, were gradually risen from One Hundred and Thirty, to above Three Hundred, advanc'd to near Four Hundred; but, after some Fluctuation, settled at about Three Hundred and Thirty, in which Condition, with little Variation, they continued till the End of this Month."

Nine days later the South Sea Bill was passed by the House of Commons by 172 votes to 55. On April 7th it was sent to the Upper House where several of their lordships made flaming attacks against it. Lords North and Grey said it was " calculated for the enriching of a few and the impoverishing of a great many; and not only made for but countenanced and authorised the fraudulent and pernicious practice of stock-jobbing, which produced irreparable mischief in diverting the genius of the people from trade and industry." The licentious twenty-two year old Duke of Wharton—son of the Wharton who had seduced Walpole's sister—often spoke with conviction on moral problems and said " that the artificial and prodigious rise of

[1] *The Political State of Great Britain.*

South Sea stock was a dangerous bait, which might decoy many unwary people to their ruin and allure them by a false prospect of gain to part with what they had got by their labour and industry to purchase imaginary riches."

Nevertheless the Bill received a large majority. Two weeks later Nathaniel Gould, a director of the Bank of England, wrote sadly to Robert Walpole. " You have heard me charged with calling this scheme a chimera. 'Tis true I did so, and sorry I am to own myself mistaken. For I could not believe that such a project (at least as it was in its original design) could ever have made entry into, much lesse have passed through the place [Parliament] I have seen it do."[1]

Now let us pause a moment and examine the role played by Robert Walpole. Had he got the right end of the stick? If his motion had been passed, forcing the company to declare the ratio of stock it would give, would the South Sea proposition have been reasonable? We can answer this by looking at the Bank proposals. No one criticised this scheme. Was it sound? No modern economist would think so. The Bank had planned to strike £15,000,000 of new stock to convert the redeemable debts; since Bank shares were selling at £150 in the market, and par value was £100, it would have been obliged to part with only £10,000,000 of stock; the £5,000,000 of surplus stock would have been sold to the public to raise the premium owed to the Government. But this money would not have been " profit" as we understand it. It would have been new capital. And unless the new capital had been put to work to expand the business of the Bank, it would have been impossible for the directors to pay dividends on the new shares; and without dividends the price of the stock eventually would drop. The same criticism, of course, applies to the South Sea Company. In this case the premium pledged to the Government was £2,000,000 higher. " Let any-one of but common understanding consider one moment, how it

[1] *Sir Robert Walpole*: J. H. Plumb, Cresset Press.

could be possible for either company to effect what they now proposed, so as not to be losers themselves, without egregiously deceiving and inuring the proprietors of these debts." Thus wrote Adam Anderson, the famous author of *The Origins of Commerce*, at the end of the eighteenth century. A more modern economist, W. R. Scott, wrote in 1911, that " the Bank was fortunate in escaping the evils that beset its great rival, for it must not be forgotten that it accepted the same principles . . ." Only one contemporary pamphleteer seems to have put his finger squarely on the weak spot. " The rise of the stock above the true capital will be only imaginary; that one added to one, by any rules of vulgar arithmetic, will never make three and a half; and that consequently all the fictitious value must be a loss to some person or other, first or last; that the only way to prevent it to oneself, must be to sell out betimes, and so let the Devil take the hindmost . . ."

The idea of credit was so new that the people of the day exaggerated its powers. Consequently the Government demanded far too high a premium for permission to carry out the scheme. One of the most extraordinary aspects of the situation, however, was the fact that " trade " with South America, the supposed business of the South Sea Company, was scarcely mentioned. Yet it was only by an increase in business, or at least the expectation of an increase in business, that stocks could be kept at a high price. A modern historian says, " Unfortunately ' South Sea ' Company is a highly misleading name, for trade with the South Seas had little to do with the project at all. It was essentially a finance company designed to take over part of the national debt." But this, too, is misleading. Simply converting the debt did not make it a finance house. Unless it employed the credit at its disposal in a profitable *business*, its share prices were bound to fall. A number of rumours were put around Exchange Alley to excite the hopes of the public; that the Assiento trade was to be restored and enlarged; that the King of Spain was willing to cede four ports in Peru in exchange for Gibraltar and Port

Mahon; that the South Sea Company was negotiating for trading rights in Africa. However most M.Ps. recognised these stories as part of the normal "jobbing tricks" practised at that time.

But to return to Robert Walpole. Why do the history books picture him as the man who foresaw and proclaimed to the world the ruin that the South Seas scheme would bring? The portrait is entirely due to his first biographer, the Archdeacon Coxe, who published an account of Walpole's life in 1798. For years historians have accepted his lead. In describing the February debates in the House of Commons, Coxe assigned to Walpole the argument that the scheme " countenanced the pernicious practice of stock jobbing, by diverting the genius of the nation from trade and industry; that it held out a dangerous lure by decoying the unwary to their ruin by a false prospect of gain, and to part with the gradual profits of their labours for imaginary wealth."

These words have a familiar ring. They are the words spoken by the Lord North and the Duke of Wharton. On what did Coxe base his information? As two of his sources, he gives the *Political State* and the *Origins of Commerce*. But there is no mention of Walpole's words in either one. As a third reference he gives the Walpole papers. Walpole's latest biographer, J. H. Plumb, recently went through these papers and declared that " at no point in these debates, for which reports exist, did Walpole attack the whole structure and policy of the South Sea Company." Why not? He was in opposition to the Government; he had no faith in the project; he saw through the South Sea Company's plans, and knew how it intended to make its "profits." Perhaps the answer lies in Walpole's relationship with the Duchess of Kendal. He had taken great pains to cultivate the King's favourite and was proud of the high favour in which she held him. She was vitally important to him, first, because she was his chief channel with St. James's Palace, and second, because her influence might pave his way back to office. The Duchess of

Kendal had received £10,000 to aid the passing of the South Sea Bill. Walpole would not have liked to incur her displeasure.

Walpole's manners were boorish, but he was shrewd and hard-headed, and played his political cards adroitly. For over two years he had worked to get back into the Government on his own terms. The very week the South Sea Act was passed his ambition was realised. The Earl of Sunderland dispatched the elder Mr. Craggs, the usual contact man, with instructions to make him an offer. Sunderland took the step reluctantly, but he was alarmed by rumours that Walpole was undermining the Government's credit with the King, through the Duchess of Kendal. He was also worried because the King had overspent his Civil List allowance by £600,000 and it was necessary to get the debts written off by Parliament; this could not be done without Walpole's help.

The offer of a job presented certain difficulties for Walpole. He had not been idle during his three years of opposition. He had made close friends with the Princess of Wales. The breach between the Prince and the King had never been healed. They had not spoken to each other for over two years. The Waleses had set up a rival court at their house in Leicester Square. Since the King had made it plain that those who frequented his son's circle would not be welcomed in his own, the Leicester Square followers consisted mainly of the Tory opposition and dissident Whigs. "Walpole was every day this winter once, if not twice, at Leicester House," wrote Lady Cowper in her diary. In many ways Walpole and the Princess were twin spirits. They saw life through the same worldly, practical eyes. "Walpole let the Prince lye with his wife which both he and the Princess knew," wrote Lady Cowper. This may have been malicious gossip, but, equally, it may have been true. Neither Walpole nor the Princess would have taken a moral stand against happenings which suited their book from a political point of view.

Although Sunderland's invitation was what Walpole had been

working for, he could not turn his back on the Prince and Princess. Walpole was only 44; he had a long life in front of him; the King would not live forever. He came to the conclusion that he could accept office only if Sunderland would co-operate with him and force the King and the Prince to heal their breach. Sunderland hated the Prince, but Walpole dug in his toes and the Earl agreed.

It was not so easy to persuade either the King or the Prince to take the necessary steps. The only person eager for a reconciliation was the Princess. She grieved for her children whom the King had taken, refusing to allow her any jurisdiction over them; it was her only hope of getting them back. Once or twice she had coaxed the Prince into making overtures to the King but he had always been rebuffed. Only a few months previously, when George had returned from Hanover, the Prince had made a gesture. " I hear that King George has arrived in England," wrote Madame. " The poor Prince of Wales, thinking to please his father, sent a page with his compliments and congratulations on his safe return, but the King refused to even hear the message, sending back the young page with bitter and scornful words."[1]

Consequently the Prince was in an ugly mood. Sunderland, Stanhope and Walpole jointly drafted a letter of submission which the Prince was to send to the King. It took all of Walpole's persuasiveness and the Princess's tears to make him do it. Whatever the outcome, he made it clear to Walpole that he flatly refused to return to St. James's Palace to live. This was lucky as the King flatly refused to have him. Indeed, for several weeks the King was so sullen at the prospect of having to consort with his son again, that no one dared approach him.

The letter was sent, and on April 23rd the King received the Prince in private. Lady Cowper received an account from the Princess which she recorded in her diary. " The Prince took his chair and went to St. James's, where he saw the King in his closet.

[1] *Letters of Madame*: Ed. Scott Stevenson.

The Prince made him a short compliment, saying it had been a great grief to him to have been in his displeasure so long; that he was infinitely obliged to H.M. for his permission of waiting upon him, and that he hoped the rest of his life would be such as the King would never have cause to complain of. The King was much dismayed, pale, and could not speak to be heard but by broken sentences, and said several times, ' *Votre conduite, votre conduite* '; but the Prince said he could not hear distinctly anything but those words. The Prince went after he had stayed about five minutes in the closet . . . the Prince came back . . . with the Beefeaters round his chair, and holloing and all marks of joy which could be shown to the multitude. He looked grave, and his eyes are red and swelled, as one has seen him upon other occasions when he is mightily ruffled. He immediately dismissed all the Company, and I was ordered to be there at five in the afternoon.

" At five I went, and found the Guards before the door, the Square full of coaches; the rooms full of company; everything gay and laughing; nothing but kissing and wishing of joy; and in short, so different a face of things, nobody could conceive that so much joy should be after so many resolutions never to come to this . . ."

The occasion was not the triumph the onlookers had hoped for. The King had done as he had promised but there was no forgiveness in his heart. He hated his son as passionately as ever. The next day, they met at Court, after attending St. James's Chapel. " When the King came out, the Prince stood by him. The King spoke to most people except the Prince; they two only looked grave and out of humour."[1]

This was the atmosphere and it continued to be the atmosphere as long as the King lived. Five years later a Frenchman who was invited to Court, wrote home, " As soon as the Princess of Wales entered the drawing room the King went to greet her, treated her most graciously, and conversed with her for some

[1] *Diary*: Lady Cowper.

time, but he did not speak to the Prince, and even avoided going near him."[1] Nevertheless, as far as appearances were concerned, the breach was healed and the dignity of the monarchy restored. In June, 1720, Walpole received his payment by becoming Paymaster General, while Townshend took office as Lord President.

[1] *A Foreign View of England*: César de Saussure.

IV

TROUBLE IN PARIS

MEANWHILE France was in an uproar. While England was pushing through its South Sea bill John Law's system was collapsing. Mississippi stock had begun to fall in January, soon after Law was made Comptroller General, and by March all sorts of disquieting rumours were sweeping Paris. Lord Stair devoured them with relish. He was packing up his belongings in the British Embassy and waiting for his successor. Still smarting under the humiliation at being sacked because of his quarrel with Mr. Law, he naturally welcomed bad news about his enemy. He was delighted when M. le Blanc, the French Minister of War, called on him and told him that the Regent was in a fury with Law because his predictions were proving false. He eagerly relayed the gossip to Mr. Craggs in London. " You may depend upon it, that Law is mightily shaken in his master's good opinion, who, within these few days past, has used him most cruelly to his face, and calling him all the names that can be thought of, knave and madman, etc. He did not know what hindered him to send him to the Bastille, and that there never was anyone sent there that deserved it so well. The Duke of Orléans was upon the close-stool when Mr. Law came in. The Duke was in such a passion that he ran to Mr. Law with his breeches about his heels and made him the compliment mentioned above . . . Law's head is so heated, that he does not sleep at nights, and has formal fits of frenzy. He gets out of bed almost every night, and runs stark staring mad about the room, making a terrible noise, sometimes singing and dancing; at other times swearing, staring, and stamping, quite out of himself. Some nights ago, his wife, who had come into the room upon the noise he made, was forced to ring the bell for people to come to her assistance. The officer of the guard was the first to come and found Law in his shirt, who had set two chairs in the middle of the room, and was dancing round them, quite out of his wits. This scene the officer of the guard told to le Blanc, from whom it came to me by a very sure conveyance."[1]

Stair's stories appear exaggerated. There is no indication that Law went "mad," and if the Regent quarrelled with him, the anger was only temporary. What is interesting about the letter is that it was written in March, 1720, a month before Parliament passed the South Sea Act. The fact that the French financial structure was in danger seems to have made no impression on British politicians. Indeed, one of the curious features of the South Sea boom is that it took place during the exact seven months that Law's system disintegrated. Mississippi stock began to fall in January 1720, when the South Sea proposals were first put to the House of Commons; and the disorder was acute by August when South Sea stock, which had tripled between January and April, gaily tripled again. Secretary Craggs, who had the benefit of Lord Stair's graphic dispatches, and who, in conjunction with his father, was heavily involved in the South Sea scheme, does not appear to have drawn the slightest parallel between the French situation and developments in England.

What *was* the French situation? What had happened?

The explanation appears simple enough to-day: in the economic jargon of our times too much money was chasing too few goods. The Government had printed hundreds of millions of paper money in order to give people the means of buying shares in Law's company. This had caused appalling inflation. The price of all commodities had rocketed. Bread, milk and meat had risen six and seven times in cost. Cloth had increased 300%. One gentleman won immortality in the history books by paying £10 for a roast chicken for his dinner.

The result of this growing inflation was to make the holders

[1] *Hardwicke State Papers.*

of Mississippi stock nervous, and in January many of the big operators decided to sell and put their gains into " real wealth." They chose the commodities which throughout the ages have been regarded as basic securities; property and gold. Of course the buyers only had bank notes to offer and in order to induce proprietors to part with land they had to offer huge paper sums; gold, whether in the form of jewellery, plate or money, fetched even more astronomical figures.

With the selling of stocks the market began to fall. Mr. Law had been Comptroller General of Finance for less than two weeks. He was at the height of his fame and influence, and was confident that if swift action was taken the deterioration could be halted. Two things must be accomplished; first, people must be prevented from turning back to gold, second, the price of shares must be stabilised.

The gold psychology was not easy to counter. The reader will recall that when Mr. Law ran the Bank of France as a private institution he had insisted on keeping a large reserve of gold so that customers could redeem their bank notes whenever they wished. He had prophesied that the day would come when paper money would be so firmly established (as it is to-day) that no one would even think of gold. At first he had admitted that this frame of mind could not be brought about quickly, then he grew over-confident; perhaps it already had been achieved. When the State took over his bank he did not insist on the gold reserve being maintained. Indeed, he agreed to the printing of hundreds of millions of livres in order to encourage the public to invest in Mississippi stock. As a result the bank had less than a 2% reserve. Naturally it could not stand even a mild demand for specie.

Law had taken a dangerous gamble. When he saw that it was not going to succeed he knew there was no time to be lost. Other means must be used to stifle the urge for gold. He called upon the Regent and prevailed upon him to issue, in the name of the King, a series of extraordinary edicts. Bank notes were declared the only legal tender; payments in gold and silver above 100 francs were prohibited; jewellery could not be worn without permission (except for ecclesiastical rings); goldsmiths were forbidden to make, use or even import plate.

This was only the beginning. A few weeks later more edicts were issued of a far more drastic and revolutionary character. France was to abolish the use of gold and silver as specie. In future it would not be employed to pay debts of any kind, not even foreign ones. Indeed, from May onwards no more gold and silver would be coined. This was not all. Mr. Law had driven gold under the counter; now his problem was to stop black market dealings and hoarding. He made impassioned speeches against hoarders, branding them enemies of the State. No person in France, no matter what his rank, would be allowed to possess gold and silver exceeding 500 livres in value. Severe penalties were attached and a pernicious system of spying was authorised. The public was invited to turn informer. All gold that was found would be confiscated and large rewards would go to those who had assisted in the discovery. The police would have the right to enter any house at any time.

It is fascinating to observe that the State capitalism of Mr. Law trod the same road which was to become only too familiar to the people of the 20th century. Despite his idealism, State capitalism meant dictatorship, and dictatorship meant the secret police. Many people were so frightened by the edict they took their gold to the bank; others decided to risk it, and a large proportion had their money confiscated. Mr. Law's appeal to the baseness of human nature was effective. Greed and spite prompted thousands of individuals to become informers. The most prevalent cases were servants against employers; but there were many instances of families dividing against each other. Brother turned against brother and son betrayed father. Although such examples have become a feature of totalitarianism in our day, they were regarded as so strange and shocking at the time, that contemporary writers beg their readers' indulgence before citing them. Apparently they were fairly frequent. When information was received the police acted swiftly, tearing up floor-boards and digging up gardens. Thousands of pounds of gold were discovered. Only the richest men emerged unscathed. The Duc de Bourbon and the Prince de Conti were known to have visited the bank early in January and driven away with carts piled high with gold. The police entered their houses but they were too frightened to search the establishments of such powerful nobles; or perhaps they were bribed. The result was that no gold was found. Other high personages did not try to resist the edicts. Apparently Madame was one, for on March 30th she wrote unhappily to her half-sister. " I think it hard lines that there is no more gold to be seen, because for forty-eight years now I have never been without some beautiful gold pieces in my pocket and now there is nothing to be had but silver coins of very little value. Monsieur Law is certainly terribly hated . . ."[1]

While the edicts against gold were tumbling out, Law was framing a scheme which would achieve his second objective; stabilising the price of Mississippi shares. A present day chartered accountant, viewing the position of his company, would throw up his hands and declare that salvation was impossible. The Company had issued 624,000 shares which had been carried by private speculation to prodigious heights. On a modest calcul-ation, taking 10,000 livres as an average share price, the capitalis-ation of the Company would amount to something in the region of 6,000,000,000 livres—or £300,000,000. The only way such a price could be maintained would be to pay dividends on this amount. But the Company did not even have an income sufficient to pay 1%. It is clear to us that whatever Mr. Law did his edifice was doomed.

However, the Comptroller was an optimist and a gambler. He decided to play one more long shot. If it came off all would be well; if it failed, all would be lost. First of all he amalgamated

[1] *The Letters of Madame*: Ed. Scott Stevenson.

bank and company and made them one institution. Then he announced that Mississippi stock would be fixed at 9,000 livres (£450) a share. A bureau of conversion would be opened where customers could either buy or sell shares, giving or receiving bank notes in exchange. Law hoped by this to dispel fear and to stop the wave of selling. If only people would hold their shares and look upon them as a long term investment, the development of the North American continent would prove so profitable, everyone would make large profits.

The drawback to his scheme was that it called for patience over scores of years. Needless to say it did not work. The fixed price, instead of putting a stop to the wave of selling, added as an inducement. The public had lost confidence; it was sure that the stock would sink much lower and thousands flocked to the bureau of conversion. This put the Company in a still more desperate position. It had sold its shares for sums ranging from 500 livres to 5,000 livres. (Prices above this amount had been paid by people dealing privately among each other.) How could it hope to buy back all its shares at 9,000? The only answer was to print more money. Once again the presses began to churn. One billion and a half livres were poured on to the market, and inflation leapt forward like an angry fire.

Up until now the Regent had not interfered with Law's plans. Although he may have had scenes with him in the early spring, when things appeared to be getting out of hand, Law's assurances had smoothed him down, and he had been relieved to turn away from the irksome business of government to the absorbing pursuit of pleasure. His drinking and carousing was growing more abandoned with the years. He had always had a profusion of mistresses, but formerly he had entertained them at private parties. Now a curious fetish had overtaken him. He insisted on making a public announcement each time he acquired a new mistress. At first he had been content merely to seat the lady in the front row of his opera box. Then the urge for public appreciation became more pronounced. Nothing but a magnificent fête would do. When a woman named Madame d'Averne succumbed to his attentions he insisted that people send her gifts, as for a wedding. To mark the event he gave a huge masked ball at St. Cloud. All the most illustrious members of the aristocracy were bidden, and the celebrations lasted until the small hours of the morning. No expense was spared. Twenty thousand lanterns illuminated the park and a spectacular display of fireworks took place at midnight. Madame d'Averne presented a belt to the Regent with great ceremony, and a poem, specially written by Voltaire, on the charms of the modern Venus, was recited aloud. Madame d'Averne's husband was present and looked immensely pleased. He had been made a captain of the guard and given a decoration, which he wore with pride. " Though all were eager to see the fête," wrote a contemporary, " there was no one who was not indignant . . . It is against religion to proclaim so publicly the triumph of vice . . ."[1]

The older generation may have been shocked, but the fashionable young ladies of the day were delighted. It made them aspire more than ever to be singled out by the Regent. One night a group of society beauties, in the same box at the opera, discovered that all of them had slept with the Regent. They accosted him brazenly and said, " Sire, behold your harem! "

Madame found these scenes distressing. She wrote countless letters deploring the modern lack of romance, and the loose conduct of her son. " Between my son and his mistresses everything is full speed ahead and with no trace of gallantry." She blamed the high-ranking ladies of the court for the sordid state of affairs, declaring that they were far more dissipated than women of the lower classes. She objected almost as strongly to their clothes as their morals. Madame de Montespan had worn loose shapeless garments, known as *robes battantes*, to hide her pregnancy; now these clothes had become the fashion. " *Robes battantes* I abhor," wrote Madame, " and will not even admit into

[1] *Journal de Barbier.*

my presence. To me they seem indecent and look as if one had got straight out of bed." Because of her firmness, ladies became reluctant to call on her. "I no longer have any circle," she complained to her half-sister in April, "because foot-stool ladies very seldom come to see me, since they cannot make up their minds to appear otherwise than in *robes battantes*. I invited them, as usual, to be present at the audience I was giving to the Ambassador from Malta but only one put in an appearance . . ."

Apart from licentiousness, morals were slipping in other directions as well. A wave of crime was sweeping Paris. It had begun at the time of the stock-market boom, when gambling and easy money had attracted almost every thief and pick-pocket in the country, and it had been increasing in volume ever since. Each day murders and robberies were reported; and the police were so busy searching for gold they could not cope with the situation. One of the most notorious figures was the master-thief Cartouche. This gentleman had been educated at one of the best schools in Paris. He had stolen money from a fellow pupil, and when he saw that it was impossible to escape detection, had run away. He stumbled on a band of gypsies and spent several years roaming about with them and learning the art of stealing. He had been caught twice and had escaped each time. His elegant manners and curious code of behaviour captured the public imagination and made him a national figure. For example, he always returned articles which might be valuable to the owner but would not fetch much money in the market. Secondly, he never robbed anyone twice. Whenever possible he presented his victim with a card of immunity. If other members of his gang should happen to fall on the same person, and he produced the card, he would be left in peace. A number of young bloods joined Cartouche's circle for the excitement. An elderly gentle-man who was robbed on his way to a dinner arrived out of breath, expostulating about his misfortune. His hostess greeted him warmly, then his eye lit on her son—none other than the thief who had assailed him. In order to avoid a scene, he said nothing.

However, a robbery was committed in the spring of 1720 which caused a sensation throughout Europe. The crime was committed by the 22-year old Count d'Horn, a kinsman of the Duc d'Orléans, and a member of a semi-royal family which belonged to one of the Low Country dynasties. Young d'Horn had come to Paris when the Mississippi boom was at its height and had fallen into bad company. Tales reached his mother that he was running up bills and she sent a gentleman from Flanders to Paris to pay off his creditors and bring him home. Unfortunately the agent arrived too late. Twenty-four hours earlier, young Count d'Horn had announced in the Rue Quincampoix that he wished to buy a large block of Mississippi shares. He had made an appointment with a stockbroker at a public house. He went there with two accomplices at the appointed time, lured the victim to a private room, stabbed him to death and ran off with his portfolio. The dying man had screamed for help, and d'Horn and one of his companions were caught. He was speedily brought to trial and sentenced to be broken on the wheel.

This announcement caused a storm of protest. Although morals were at a discount, standards of etiquette and procedure were rigidly maintained; any deviation could provoke emotional upheavals of a most profound order. Few people objected to the count paying the death penalty. But the wheel normally was reserved for low-born criminals. You could shoot, hang or guillotine an aristocrat, but not break him on the wheel. Several angry members of the d'Horn family called on the Duc de Saint-Simon and asked him to use his influence with the Regent. The duke was sympathetic for he believed that aristocrats were a breed apart, and their privileges should be scrupulously observed.

" They explained that the mode of execution of a criminal was very important in the Low Countries and Germany; death by beheading carried with it no stigma on his family, whereas death on the wheel was considered infamous, and would disqualify his near relations and their descendants for three generations for admission to any noble chapter. This, to say nothing of the shame, was very detrimental to a noble family, for it prevented the daughters from becoming canonesses, and the sons from aspiring to any of the sovereign bishoprics. This plea had some weight with me and I promised to do my best with the Regent. I represented to him that he might satisfy the just demands of the public, and at the same time spare the honour of an illustrious house, by commuting Count d'Horn's penalty at the last moment to death by the axe; if he allowed it to be carried out he would drive the numerous connections of the family to despair, for the matter would be raked up again every time a vacancy arose in a noble chapter; and indeed Count d'Horn's sister was just on the point of being received into one.

" The Duke of Orléans said he thought I was right, and the penalty should be commuted. I then took leave of him, warning him at the same time not to let Dubois and Law argue him out of his decision: for, the safety of stock-jobbers being essential to the maintenance of credit, they were bent on severity. Then I went to La Ferté, to spend Holy Week in retirement. It turned out just as I had anticipated: the first piece of news that reached me from Paris was that Count d'Horn and his accomplice had expired on the wheel on the 26th of March, having been previously subjected to torture. All the distinguished nobility of the Low Countries and Germany resented the execution as an outrage, and some curious plots for vengeance on the Duke of Orléans were concocted. Long after his death some members of the Horn family spoke of him to me in terms of the bitterest resentment."[1]

Count d'Horn's crime gave John Law an excuse for closing down the activities of the Rue Quincampoix. The street, he said, had lost the reason for its existence. Since a bureau of conversion was functioning, there was no further need for private dealing. An edict followed, which not only forbade

[1] *Memoirs of the Duc de Saint-Simon*: Edited by Francis Arkwright, Stanley Paul & Co.

speculation in the Quincampoix, but in any part of Paris. This did not put the brokers out of business, but drove them underground. " The police kept a vigilant lookout for merchants and brokers dealing in public securities. A group of men would gather in some place, shares would be offered, bids made, bargains consummated. Suddenly the cry would be heard, " The watch! " Instantly operators, merchants, clerks, would disperse and seek escape by the alleys and courtyards, like a band of mischievous boys . . ."[1]

These measures, of course, did nothing to halt the inflation. The huge sums of paper money which had been printed so that Law's company could buy back the Mississippi shares through the bureau of conversion, had sent the prices of commodities rocketing still further. Anger against Mr. Law was deepening, and the Regent was blamed as well. In parts of Paris people were bordering on starvation and there was ominous talk of a revolution. Certain members of the aristocracy were taking advantage of the situation and behaving in a shameless fashion. " Three dukes, belonging to the highest families, have done something which I consider degrading," wrote Madame. " The Duc d'Antin, the Duc d'Estrées and the Duc de la Force; the first one has bought up all the cloth in order to sell it more dearly; the second all the coffee and chocolate; and the third has done even worse because he has bought up all the candles and has made them exorbitant in price . . ."[2]

John Law realised with a shock that the battle against gold was no longer his chief problem. Inflation was his real enemy. At the end of May he made a desperate attempt to lower the prices of provisions. His plan was announced to the world in an edict, issued on May 21st, which is famous in history as the climax of his struggle to prevent his " system " from collapsing. The edict stated that too much money was in circulation; this

[1] *France under the Regency*: James Breck Perkins.
[2] *Letters of Madame*: Ed. Scott Stevenson.

was causing the price of provisions to rise. The only way to reduce costs was to withdraw part of the currency. This would have to be done by devaluation. Consequently bank notes and Mississippi shares would gradually be reduced in value over the next few months. The 100 livre note would be worth 80 livres in a week's time, 70 in a fortnight, 60 in three weeks, until it finally was pegged at 50, half its present value. The same schedule would be followed until shares worth 9,000 came down to 5,000.

This plan was the only sensible way to try and deal with the strange, unknown disease of inflation. If it had been adopted people would have been no worse off than they already were, and there might have been some hope of an improvement in the future; if the State could force down prices the 50 livre note might have the same purchasing power as the 100 livre note. But the public did not view it in this light. A 100 livre note did not buy much, but a 50 livre note would buy only half as much.

Such a howl of rage went up from the public, it was feared that the streets would soon be running in blood. Menacing crowds gathered outside the Palais Royal and there were demonstrations in many parts of Paris. Overnight Law became the most hated man in the Kingdom. He was depicted as a monster of treachery and dishonesty. When he had launched his bank notes he had promised solemnly that they would never be devalued. Now he had broken his word.

The anger of the populace, however, went deeper than this. Law had been the idol of the nation. Despite the crises of the past few months many people still had faith in his genius; they clung to the hope that somehow he would produce a miracle and pull them out of their difficulties. Now their last illusion was shattered. He had no remedy. He had failed them. His only prescription was to strip them of their last remaining possessions. The ugly mood of the public was so frightening that the Government withdrew the edict in a week's time; and Law was removed from the office of Comptroller General.

For some weeks his position was a matter of wild conjecture. All sorts of rumours began to circulate. Some people insisted that the edict had been issued by Law's enemies, in the Council of Finance, without his knowledge; and that he had resigned his office in protest. This argument was bolstered by the fact that he still remained a director of bank and company. Other people said the Regent was disgusted with him, and would reveal his displeasure to the world by flinging him into the Bastille.

Neither theory was correct. The truth was far simpler. The Government had approved the edict of May 21st, which had originated with Law; it had not expected the decree to be applauded but it was completely taken aback by the fury of the public reaction. The Regent could not afford to share Law's unpopularity. He had sacrificed his minister to appease his subjects. Publicly he refused to receive Law; privately he welcomed him up the back stairs.

The edict of May 21st marks the virtual end of the " system." Law had no more solutions to offer. The only way back to solvency was the rough, orthodox road with its high toll of casualties. From June onwards gold was accepted once again as the basis of the currency. The edicts prohibiting its use and possession were withdrawn. Anyone could have as much gold and silver as he could lawfully obtain. " Alas," wrote a contemporary, " the permission comes when nobody has any left." The menacing mood of the population prompted the Government to try and relieve the lot of the poorest people. It was announced that the 10 livre note, the denomination held mostly by working people, would be redeemed in gold. Huge crowds assembled outside the bank in the Rue Vivienne. Gold was in such short supply that the doors were opened for only three hours each day. Long queues gathered at two in the morning, and waited all night until the doors were opened at nine. At noon thousands of starving and desperate people were turned away. On June 11th Madame wrote to her half-sister in a futile, in-

John Law, founder of the Mississippi Company, whose brilliant but over-ambitious financial schemes brought France to ruin

sensitive vein. "The working people no longer want to work, and they put a price on their goods three times higher than they are now worth because of the bank-notes. I have often wished that these bank-notes were consigned to hell-fire." The next day she wrote more explicitly. "Judging from the universal uproar, it seems that things are going terribly badly. I should wish to see Law go to the Devil with his system, and wish that he had never set foot in France."[1]

On July 17th, a hot, stifling night, the largest crowd that had ever collected waited in front of the bank. By three in the morning there were fifteen thousand hungry and determined people. It was a swaying, jostling, shouting crowd; burly men tried to force their way forward and women screamed and kicked. A group of boys climbed a tree and swung themselves over a good many heads, by the branches. When the morning light came it was found that sixteen people had been suffocated.

The crowd was appalled by the calamity. It was born of their suffering, and they were determined to make their resentment felt. Some of them marched to the Louvre and demonstrated outside the windows of the young King. But most of them went to the Palais Royal and called for the Regent. They carried four corpses on stretchers and shouted to him to come and see what his Government had brought about. When the officials saw the huge throngs gathering, they called out soldiers and police. Monsieur le Blanc, the Minister of War, came out on the steps and begged the people to preserve law and order. He displayed great bravery, for a false move could have sparked off a general uprising. Gradually the throng began to melt away. While a number of them were still assembled, however, John Law's carriage drove through their midst. His livery was recognised. "A woman cried out to him, 'If there were four more women like myself, you would be torn to pieces.'" It seemed probable that such would be his fate, but by his self-possession Law succeeded in keeping the crowd at bay, and made

[1] *The Letters of Madame:* Ed. Scott Stevenson

his escape by a back door of the palace. The carriage was over-turned, and the coachman had his leg broken. Law remained in concealment at the Palais Royal for ten days. His family, as well as himself, were in danger from the hostility of the mob. His daughter, a child of thirteen, was in her carriage when some ruffian cried out, " That is the livery of the beggar who doesn't pay his ten franc bills." The carriage was pelted with mud, and the girl received slight injuries. Madame de Torcy was taken for Law's wife by some peasants, and they were about to drown her in a neighbouring pond. Only by proving her identity could she escape their violence."[1]

It was no longer safe for Law or any member of his family to drive through the streets of Paris. The Duc de Bourbon, who owed his millions to Law's " system," came to his rescue. He took Lady Catherine Law, her young daughter and sixteen year old son under the protection of his roof at St. Maur. Law, himself, remained at the Palais Royal for ten days, then retired to one of his country houses at St. Cloud.

He was dazed and helpless. Ever since the fatal edict of May 21st he had been suffering from shock. His " system " had failed. It represented the thought and work of a lifetime; now there was nothing for him to do but stand by and watch the great edifice crumble to the ground. He still had audiences with the Regent who was at his wits' end to know how to handle the situation. But Law had no more proposals to make. His theories lay in ruins. Worse still, he was accused of having contrived the disaster. He could not get used to his unpopularity. Only six months before he had been the most brilliant figure in Europe; his daughter's hand had been sought by the most illustrious families, his son had been invited to dance in a ballet with the King. Every mark of esteem had been shown him; now he was blamed and despised. The reins of the Government were in the hands of the Abbé Dubois. He was almost a pariah.

The July riots appear to have affected his brain. For some

[1] *France under the Regency*: James Breck Perkins.

weeks, according to Madame, he was overcome by terror. His fear was not altogether imaginary, but apart from the wrath of the mob he knew enough of the unreliability of the Government to realise that the Regent's advisers might mark him down for further sacrifice. An off-chance remark could send him to the Bastille, or even result in the guillotine. Madame was at St. Cloud in August, not far from Mr. Law's residence, and in almost every letter mentions the Scot in derisory tones. On August 17th, " Law is like a dead man and his face is as white as a sheet. He has not been able to get over the latest frights he has had . . ."; the next day, " All is quiet here still, but Mr. Law dare not stir out of his house. The women from the market have placed little boys as spies all round his house in order to know when he comes out. That doesn't promise well for him and I am afraid there may be a new uprising "; three days later, " Never in my life have I seen any Englishman or Scotchman so cowardly as Law. Prosperity must have taken away his courage, because it is not easy to give up one's possessions. I expect there are times when he wishes he were on the Mississippi or in Louisiana."[1]

Madame's bitterness towards the financier is not difficult to understand. He had brought discredit on her son, and she could not forgive him for it. The Regent was almost as hated as his fallen minister. People were reviving the incest stories about himself and his daughter, the Duchesse de Berri, and every morning rude slogans were scribbled on the palace walls. " I have neither good nor evil to say of Mr. Law's system," wrote Madame in one of her calmer moments, " because it is quite incomprehensible to me, but when I see all the worry and harm it has brought my son, I could wish that it had never been thought of. When people are as self-interested as the French are, from Monsieur le Duc down to the meanest lackey, one is never safe when there is anything to be gained by one's death. For which reason I am very anxious, and alarmed for my son's life. As far as

[1] *Letters of Madame*: Ed. Scott Stevenson.

I myself am concerned I have nothing to dread, because my death would benefit no one. Would to God that I had myself to worry about. I should not have a moment's fear.

" There is still a great deal of money in France, but every one conceals it from selfishness, and won't put it into circulation. They take no notice of the laws Monsieur Law made on the subject. No one has any taste for war here, but they are very fond of luxury, which has never been indulged in to such an extent as it is at present. Time will show what will be the result."[1]

This was France in the summer of 1720. Let us cross the channel and see what was happening in England.

[1] *The Letters of Madame:* Ed. Scott Stevenson.

V

LONDON GOES MAD

A few days after the South Sea Act was passed Mr. John Blunt did a very peculiar thing. He announced that on the 14th of April twenty thousand South Sea shares would be sold to the public. This had nothing to do with converting the national debt; the shares were not to be exchanged for the securities held by Government creditors. It was simply a cash transaction.

In view of the fact that the only shares which the South Sea Company was legally entitled to sell were surplus shares this was a strange beginning; how could a surplus be determined in advance? The South Sea Company had been authorised by Parliament to issue one South Sea share for every £100 of debt converted; to put it another way, if £600 of debt was converted the Company could issue six shares. However if the market value of South Sea stock was quoted at £300 a share at the time of the transaction the Company would have to part with only two shares; the four remaining shares would constitute the surplus.

By offering shares to the public before the conversion Mr. Blunt was banking on the fact that the stock market price would remain at its present high quotation. What he was doing was scarcely ethical yet both Parliament and Press seemed oblivious to it, for not the slightest criticism was levelled against him. On the other hand, Mr. Blunt had every reason for optimism. There was such a rush for shares on April 14th that the issue was sold for £300 a share within a few hours; furthermore, instead of twenty thousand shares being sold, twenty-two and a half thousand were disposed of. This was stated to have been an oversight. It was explained that " the subscription was taken in several books to prevent crowding, notwithstanding which the crowd was so great that the clerks had not an opportunity of communicating with each other." The success of the operation encouraged Blunt to repeat it; on the 30th of April a second subscription of ten thousand shares was sold, this time for £400 a share. Once again the same confusion reigned, with the result that five thousand extra shares were put on the market.

Mr. Blunt was pleased with life. His financial triumphs brought him the first social success he had ever known. Overnight he had become the toast of London. He had moved into a luxurious house in the West End with his dreary, down-trodden wife, a daughter of an ex-Governor of Bengal, and was revelling in his sudden prestige. Mrs. Blunt was terrified by the grandeur of the invitations they received, which ranged from Court levees to ducal balls. But Mr. Blunt accepted them as well-deserved recognition, and decided to hold levees of his own. He realised that his popularity was based on the favours he could do; all directors of the South Sea Company had shares at their disposal and could allot them to whomever they pleased. This enhanced his pleasure, for it increased his sense of power. He had an original approach to "stockjobbing." His partiality for the Bible clothed his efforts to boost South Sea stock with Christian fervour. He insisted that the more the public paid for its shares, the more it would benefit. " 'Twas his maxim, a thousand times repeated, that the advancing by all means of the price of the stock was the only way to promote the good of the Company."

Mr. Blunt bought himself a new carriage and drove regularly to South Sea House, a fine edifice at the corner of Threadneedle Street in " the City." The change that had taken place in this sedate, masculine world since his scheme had been accepted was astonishing. The quiet streets, staid merchants and dignified clerks had been inundated by a feverish invasion led by the magnificent carriages and liveried servants of the fashionable world and followed by a mêlée of farmers on horseback, town dwellers from the provinces, intellectuals, actresses, whores, servants, and sharpers of every description. The flood had begun in March when the South Sea Act looked like a certainty. Occasionally a note of warning was sounded by the newspapers but no one paid any attention. " Our South Sea Stock has made such a consumed Noise of late," declared the *Weekly Journal* on March 26th, " to the terror of the trading part of this Nation, that it has brought over many of the Quincampoix gentry to try their fortunes here; and 'tis said that abundance of our country gentlemen and rich farmers are upon the roads from several parts of the Kingdom all expecting no less than to ride down again every man in his coach and six; but, if a friend's advice is worth anything, let them take care, for though there are some prizes, they may find many more blanks, and they may happen to lose all that in an hour in Exchange Alley, which the industry and care of their ancestors has been scraping together for some ages . . ."

Exchange Alley was a narrow cobbled lane that ran between Lombard and Cornhill Streets. It was here that the stockbrokers had their offices, here that the crowds came to do their business. Speculating in shares had become the gambling craze of the country. The first " boom " in the history of England was well under way. In May Lord Oxford's brother, Mr. Edward Harley, wrote to a friend, " There are few in London that mind anything but the rising and falling of stocks."

There was only one cloud on Mr. Blunt's horizon. That was the fact that thousands of buyers were investing their money in ventures other than the South Sea. The shares of all the joint-stock companies in England were moving upward in the general enthusiasm. Furthermore, dozens of new companies were being launched each month. This trend had started a year earlier inspired by the success of Mr. Law's Mississippi Company. The South Sea Act had provided a powerful new impetus and during April and May alone fifty new companies had been launched.

Almost all these new concerns were illegal. No one could float a joint-stock company without a charter from the King.

Charters took time and money to acquire, and promoters were unwilling to stand by idly and miss the boom, so they were openly flaunting the law. Mr. Blunt did not approve. He could not bear to see money which he had ear-marked for the South Sea being deftly channelled away. He was determined to force the " bubble companies," as they were called, to shut up shop. He therefore persuaded the Government to set up a Parliamentary committee to investigate the situation and had every hope that action would be taken against them in a few weeks' time.

In the meanwhile promoters and speculators continued merrily on their way. Despite rumours of impending prosecutions they gambled their money with increasing abandon. Each morning the *Daily Post*, a spirited, four-page newspaper, published notices of enticing new ventures. The coffee houses, which dotted the City, lent their premises to promoters as meeting places. The owners did a huge trade and were thrilled with the opulence of many of their new customers. They bowed low to the rich gentlemen in lace and velvet and powdered wigs; and they were fascinated by the entry of expensive, crinolined females; up till now no woman—well-bred or otherwise—ventured into the City. This innovation was commemorated by the following verse:

> *Our greatest ladies hither come*
> *And ply in chariots daily;*
> *Oft pawn their jewels for a sum*
> *To venture in the Alley.*
> *Young harlots too from Drury Lane*
> *Approach the Change in coaches*
> *To fool away the gold they gain*
> *By their impure debauches.*

Despite the jibes of the ballad writers, the females added to the general excitement and the coffee houses rang with laughter and talk, as everyone discussed the latest bargains. If you had bought the *Daily Post* of April 22nd this is what you would have read:

Whereas permits were delivered out yesterday at the Salutation Tavern in Nicholas Lane in Lombard Street for shares in a sum of 1,000,000 l. sterling for effectually carrying out the African trade. Such permits will this day continue to be deliver'd out in the said trade at 2s. 6d. each share (or per 1,000 l) which shall be return'd in case this undertaking should not be carried out . . .

This day books are open'd at Mulford's Coffee House next door to the Crown Tavern behind the Royal Exchange, for completing the subscription of Two Millions for insuring all sorts of Goods & Effects from Theft and Robberies, both by Sea and Land . . .

Whereas books were open'd Monday the 18th Instant for raising a Joint Stock Company of 1,500,000 l. to be divided into shares for the effectually carrying on a Grand American Fishery, at the Ship & Castle Tavern in Cornhill. This is therefore to give Notice to all the Gentlemen concern'd that the Subscription is now compleat . . .

This day Books will be open'd at the Virginia Coffee House near the Royal Exchange at three in the afternoon, for a Subscription of 2,000,000 l. sterling for the advancement of the woollen manufacture etc. which will effectually employ all the Poor of Great Britain and be of great Advantage to the proprietors . . .

Whereas a proposition was advertised in this paper on Saturday and Monday last, for taking in Subscriptions at the Marine Coffee House in Birchin Lane for Ten Millions of Money for carrying on the Trade of the Royal Fishery. This is therefore to aquaint the Publick that the said subscription was entirely compleated on Tuesday last . . .

Pursuant to Notice given in this paper of Wednesday the 20th Instant this is to acquaint all persons concern'd in the Subscription toward carrying on a Trade to the Bay of Cappeachy that the Banker's man will attend at the Virginia Coffee House to receive 4s per cent. . . .

Several merchants and others being desirous of raising a Joint Stock Company for carrying on a Trade to Russia; this is to give notice that a Book will be open'd this day at the Globe Tavern at 11 in the forenoon, to take a Subscription of One Million Sterling in order to carry on that Trade . . .

Whereas it was advertis'd yesterday in the paper that a meeting of the subscribers to the Barbary & African Trade was to be this day at the Ship & Castle Tavern in Cornhill it is for very good reasons deferr'd; therefore the Subscribers are desir'd to meet at the same place Monday next . . .

Whereas Books were open'd yesterday at Mulford's Coffee House behind the Royal Exchange for taking in a Subscription to erect Colonies, & settle a trade to New Britannia, & some other places; and as several evil disposed persons gave themselves a great deal of trouble to discourage the said undertaking by falsely aspersing the Proprietor thereof, because he would not permit them to be concern'd therein, these are to give Notice, that notwithstanding all they could do, 700,000 1 (the part of the 2,000,000 l.) is subscribed, and on Monday next the Books will be open'd again at the same place to compleat the same; and to remove all Doubts the undertaker hereof will take no subscription Money until the same is compleated . . .

As the weeks progressed a large number of the projects became increasingly improbable. It was plain that ideas were growing both extravagant and infectious. Any novelty could be sure of finding an imitator within a few days. In May a concern was launched for reclaiming the " fen lands "; a few days later (on May 27th) this notice appeared: " whereas there are vast tracts of bogey lands in the Kingdom of Ireland, which are altogether useless and barren, Subscriptions will be taken this day, the 27th instant, at 10 in the forenoon, at the King's Head Tavern in Swithen's Alley in Cornhill for raising 3,000,000 l. sterling to purchase and drain the said bogs . . . N.B. That it may be upon a legal establishment, application will be made for a Charter." In June, the projects were even wilder. A company was formed " for extracting silver from lead " and a week later (on June 14th) the *Daily Post* announced: " Proposals for raising of Two Millions for effecting the Transmutation of Fluid Mercury or Quicksilver, into a solid and malleable Body, so that 'twill spread under the Hammer, and be of equal Use, Beauty and Value with the purest standard Silver; pursuant to which, Permits will begin to be deliver'd out, and continue till compleated, tomorrow, being the 15th instant, at the Fountain Tavern, Stocks-Market, from the hours of 12 till 3, paying 6d. per cent. for the Permit, as a Gratuity for the Projector and Company. N.B. 'Tis demonstrable by a just calculation, that each subscriber will get above 800 per cent. When full, shall open the Books, and proceed to chuse a Governor and Directors."

The wits of the day often found the situation irresistible and inserted notices in the *Daily Post* giving fictitious meeting places and announcing subscriptions " for an engine to move the South Sea House to Moorgate," or more prophetically for " the melting down of sawdust and chips and casting them into clean deal boards, without cracks or knots." However, their ingenuity was often surpassed by the genuine article. Consider the following:

For importing a large number of large jackasses from Spain to improve the breed of British Mules.

For building ships against pirates.

For insuring all masters and mistresses the losses they may sustain by servants.

For a wheel of perpetual motion.

For an immediate expeditious and cleanly manner of emptying necessary houses throughout England at a cost of £2,000,000.

For insuring marriage against divorce.

For planting of mulberry trees and breeding of silk-worms in Chelsea Park.

The unlikeliness and variety of these projects inspired a print-seller by the name of Bowles to put out " A new Pack of Bubble Cards containing 52 copper Cuts of Bubbles; with a satirical Epigram upon the same; Price 2s. 6d." This gave the humorists far more scope. A subscription taken at the Ship Tavern for trading in hair " being a commodity whose consumption is equal to, if not exceeds most of the necessaries used in dress by both sexes," inspired the following verse:

> *Here Dirty, Brown, Dark, Red and Yellow Hair*
> *Are Bleached to Colours that are Fine and Fair*
> *Then blended so, that half the whores in Town*
> *Contribute to adorn one Addl'd Crown.*

Another subscription, taken at the Fleece Tavern for " Puckle's Machine Gun " which, it was claimed, had the ability of discharging " round and square cannon balls and bullets thus making a total revolution of the art of war " (on the basis that round bullets would be used against Christians and square against Turks), drew forth the following verse:

> *A Rare invention to destroy the Crowd*
> *Of fools at Home instead of Foes Abroad*
> *Fear not, my friends, this terrible machine;*
> *They're only wounded who have shares therein.*

It would be wrong to give the impression that all the "bubbles" launched in the winter and spring of 1720 were fraudulent or lunatic. Before April the great bulk dealt with fisheries and insurance; before June with foreign trade; after that with woollen and cloth manufactures. An amusing feature of these projects is that many, which no doubt sounded strange at the time, eventually managed to work their way into our economy. Look at these: "for paying pensions to widows and others at a small discount"; "for assuring an increasing children's fortunes"; "for the furnishing of funerals to any part of Great Britain"; "for erecting houses or hospitals for taking in and maintaining illegitimate children." Such projects as "making oil from sunflower seeds," "for making salt water fresh," "for wrecks to be fished for" are no longer strange to our ears. Even a "wheel of perpetual motion" may become a reality in the atomic age.

The less exotic proposals drew great support from the aristocracy and gentry, who not only speculated but often promoted. The Prince of Wales set the fashion by becoming governor of the Welsh Copper Company. Mr. Robert Walpole tried to dissuade him, telling him that the Company's shares would be hawked about Exchange Alley as "the Prince of Wales' Bubble." This proved to be the case but the Prince did not care, as long as the stock shot up—which it did. Two other companies, known as Lord Onslow's and Lord Chetwynd's Bubbles had moved into a more exalted sphere in April, when they received a charter from the sovereign in return for their payment of £600,000 which went to pay the King's debts. The Duke of Bridgewater promoted a company to build houses in London and Westminster; the Duke of Chandos launched Yorks Building Company; the Duke of Portland contented himself with investing heavily in South Sea stock. Most speculators, however, spread their risks and bought shares in half a dozen companies. Since all shares were sold on margin and only an infinitesimal down payment was required—sometimes 1% or even lower—there was great scope for gambling. A country gentleman by the name of Mr. Rowley provides us with a sample of a day's buying. His bill-folder was stolen, and he advertised for its return in the *Daily Post* on May 11th. " Picked out of a Pocket Thursday May 5th about Jonathan's Coffee House in Exchange Alley, a black letter-case where was the following receipts. No 294 for Bricks and Tiles one share. No 1105 for Whale Fishing in Davis Straights £1,000. No 125 from the Grand Lessees of Mines Royal Mineral and Battery and for smelting of Ores, £1,000. No 37 to Thomas Dyer Esq. for making raw silk, signed J. Carleton £1,000. With several other papers of no use but to the owner. Whoever brings them to Mr. Rowley at Jonathan's Coffee House in Exchange Alley, or to Jonathan Wilde in the Old Bailey shall have two guineas reward. N.B. They are all stopped at the books."

The poor people were the ones who were taken in by the fraudulent projects. Stocks were sold to them with down payments of only 6d. or 1s. They seem to have been surprisingly gullible. The most incredible fraud was perpetrated by a Cornhill printer who announced that money would be raised for " a Company for carrying on an undertaking of Great Advantage but no one to know what it is." The printer insisted on the high sum of a £2 deposit for each share; but he gave value for money, for he promised, in return for each deposit, an annual income of £100. He took subscriptions in his office and at the end of the day had collected £2,000. That night he wisely packed his bags and disappeared.

Why did the British public gamble so recklessly and fail to draw a lesson from the financial collapse taking place in France at this precise moment? An eighteenth-century historian declares that " the people of Great Britain were as mad as a man would be thought who, seeing another fall from a precipice, shall run after him and perish in a like manner." But the truth was that the British public was not aware that France had fallen from a precipice, because of the lack of information in their press. Facts were reported briefly and critically, but there was no attempt to analyse them. " We have little money stirring here," wrote the Paris correspondent of the *Daily Post* on April 4th, " and nothing is now to be got in the Rue Quincampoix; country people run with as much precipitancy from Paris as ever they flocked to it. Provisions grow every day more dear; and as the stock-jobbing is over, multitudes who came hither with no less prospect than getting of estates, find it very difficult to get bread."

One realises with a jolt that no one understood the causes of the French misfortune. Credit was a splendid new invention, but inflation was an unrecognised and undiagnosed disease. Mr. Law and his " system " were the talk of Europe. He had saved France from bankruptcy; if, after two years, things were suddenly taking a turn for the worse, it surely was not his fault. This feeling is reflected by English writers throughout the spring of 1720, as Mississippi stock fell, edicts poured forth, supplies dried up and rioting took place in Paris. When rumours reached London that the French were blaming Mr. Law for their hardships, the British press was seized by a frenzy of patriotism. The *Weekly Journal* scarcely would admit that there were any hardships. " Nothing is more evident than that Mr. Law has been of a universal service to France," it declared on June 11th, " and that by his genius alone he has retrieved the loss of the late long and miserable war, and put the sinking credit of the nation in such a flourishing condition as was never known before . . ."

What is difficult to realise is that even as late as July when the " system " was nearing its end (and South Sea Stock was at its highest peak) the English newspapers were unable to assess the situation, or to draw any sensible conclusions.[1] *The Weekly Journal* was forced to admit that France was having difficulties, but

[1] The monthly Journal entitled *The Political State of Great Britain*, which reported the proceedings of Parliament, ran a number of " economic " articles. Most of those dealing with France, however, were merely an exposition of Mr. Law's theories.

that was as far as it would go. " ' Tis true indeed," it observed angrily on July 23rd, " the French have been, and are in some confusion; and as the case has been in other places, their commerce has been stagnated, their credit sunk, and their cash amassed in the hands of the Government; but then it is true, that none of this has been owing to Mr. Law and it is certain that the retrieving of all these unhappy circumstances must be by Mr. Law's management alone or they will still be plunging into such further difficulties as none but so superior a genius will be able to extricate them out of."

The fact that English politicians and writers refused to blame Mr. Law for the manipulation of Mississippi stock, must have been comforting to John Blunt. The cardinal principle underlying Law's operations had been " credit "; to make money so cheap that people could borrow freely to buy more and more Mississippi stock. This kept forcing the price up; whenever it looked like dropping more money was printed and more buying took place. Mr. Blunt had no printing presses, but he intended to pattern himself on Mr. Law. If necessary he would issue loans so that people could buy South Sea stock just as easily as the Parisians had bought Mississippi.

Mr. Blunt was the leading spirit of the Committee which had been set up in January to ensure the passage of the South Sea Act. Its original task was to place inducements in the right hands. Once a person had agreed to give the South Sea Company his support in return for a " reward," a block of South Sea stock, at the current market price, was entered in a secret book and credited to his name. After the passing of the Act, when the stock was 300% higher, a date was selected on which the stocks were marked as sold. The difference between the two prices was the money due to the supporter. The fact that the stocks assigned as bribes never existed was incidental. The total owed amounted to £1,250,000. It was a large sum but Mr. Blunt did not regret it. It had achieved its purpose, and there was plenty more money to come.

Sir John Blunt, prime mover in the Company's negotiations to take over the National Debt. After the Company's spectacular failure he was regarded as the chief culprit

The twenty-eight directors of the South Sea Company (apart from those on the Committee) took care not to look too closely into the junto's activities. They must have heard rumours of bribes but they were not shown " the secret book " and preferred not to be made accomplices. Four of the directors were members of Parliament; six had Government jobs; the remainder were bankers and merchants who served on many other company boards as well. They congratulated the Committee on its success in getting the South Sea Bill through Parliament and voted unanimously that it should continue to guide the Company's affairs. Thus Mr. Blunt's leadership remained unchallenged.

The chief reason for taking the two cash subscriptions in April were first to pay off the bribes, and second to introduce the scheme of loaning out money to stockholders. The Committee met to consider the position. Over thirty-seven thousand shares had been sold for a total of £12,750,000. However, since the stock had been bought on the hire-purchase plan with only a small down payment (the rest to come in two-monthly instalments over the year) only £2,750,000 was actually in hand. After the bribes were paid this left a million and a half pounds.

Here is where Mr. Blunt stepped in. Although some members of the Committee were in favour of setting a sum aside to meet part of the £7,500,000, promised to the Government, Blunt said no. He had better uses for the money. It was essential, he insisted, to push the stock as high as possible before the Company made the offer to convert the annuities. The higher the price, the less stock the Company would have to part with.

Everyone saw the sense of Mr. Blunt's argument, but how could it be done? Mr. Blunt had a startling plan based on Mr. John Law's methods. Law had raised the price of Mississippi stock by encouraging the Government to print money and lend it so cheaply that people were induced to continue buying. Blunt had no printing press, but he believed the same result would be achieved if the South Sea Company lent money to its shareholders.

This ingenious idea was received with enthusiasm. Consequently an announcement was made that loans would be issued to holders of South Sea stock; £250 could be borrowed on every £100 of stock held, but no single person could borrow more than £5,000. Here was a straight gamble which appealed to many people. Over £1,000,000 was borrowed and spent, and South Sea stock rose to 400.

On May 19th an offer was made to the annuitants. Despite all the fears and arguments expressed in the House of Commons that the Company might not make an attractive enough proposal to interest annuitants, the terms were considered so good that half the annuitants stepped forward to convert. This is what it amounted to. If you were receiving a " long " annuity of £100 a year, how much capital did it represent? It really was anyone's guess. The Government had fixed the amount at £2,000 or, in financial language, at " 20 years purchase." The Bank in its original offer to Parliament had fixed it at £1,700 (17 years purchase) but had offered to give Bank stock that was, in fact, worth £2,500 in the market. Now the South Sea Company came forward and said it would give 32 years purchase which fixed the amount at £3,200. This is the way you would be paid. You would receive £500 in bonds and cash, and 7 shares of South Sea stock which was selling in the open market at £400 per share. Thus if you cared to capitalise your annuity you could get £3,300 for it. On the other hand, if you believed in the future of the Company, and thought that stocks were going still higher, or large dividends would be paid, you would hold on. The choice was yours. Whatever you did, it looked as though your income, from now on, would be much more than £100 a year.

The terms offered to the annuitants gave the stock a spurt, for people realised that the Company would have another large surplus to sell. Although the 7 shares of South Sea stock given to each £100-annuitant represented £2,800 on the market, they only cost the Company £700. From May 19th to June 2nd the stock rose to £800 a share.

At this point there was a sharp drop, due to a wave of profit taking. The King and his entourage were leaving for Hanover. Most of them sold their stocks for ready cash. The King had bought £20,000 worth of shares in the first subscription; he parted with them for £106,500 which gave him a clear profit of over £86,000.[1] No one knows the sums made by other members of his entourage, but undoubtedly they were considerable. The drop in South Sea prices encouraged the Committee to accelerate its policy of lending money for the purchase of more stock. Between May 19th and June 14th a further £3,500,000 was spent in this way; and on June 14th the stock was selling at 750.

Now let us look at the Company balance sheet on June 14th Two cash subscriptions had been taken, in which over thirty-seven thousand shares had been sold. The money in hand (apart from that owing in instalments) amounted to £3,500,000. But here is the money spent:

Bribes	£1,250,000
Money owing in cash and bonds to annuitants	£2,700,000
Money lent	£4,500,000
Total	£8,450,000

The credit of the South Sea Company was strained to the tune of £5,000,000. In addition to this, no provision had been made to pay the Government the £7,500,000 for the privilege of putting the scheme into operation. It therefore was decided on June 15th to offer the public a third cash subscription. Fifty thousand shares would be put on the market at £1000 a share. This was the most grandiose proposal of the lot. Furthermore the shares were being offered at 25% higher than the current price. However the terms were very attractive. A down payment of 10% or £100 a share was all that was required. The rest of the money would be accepted in instalments of 10% at six-

[1] *Sir Robert Walpole*: J. H. Plumb.

month intervals, over the next four and a half years. People willing to gamble on the price going still higher decided to risk it. The whole issue was sold out in a few days and the Company received £5,000,000 in cash.

Instead of trying to balance its books, however, the Committee decided to go on lending. A plan was in hand to convert the rest of the annuities in August and it was essential to keep the share prices high. The whole five million was spent on loans. Consequently the stock reached £1050 at the end of June. The South Sea books were closed at the end of July. Parliament rose, and Mr. Blunt took his family to Tunbridge Wells; he needed a rest and an opportunity to think things over.

South Sea stock was the most fashionable speculation ever to grip Great Britain. The list of purchasers represent a sparkling galaxy of aristocrats and country squires; of members of Parliament and Cabinet ministers; of merchants and bankers. There was scarcely an upper-class family in the land that remained aloof. The whole of the oligarchy was committed. Even impoverished intellectuals borrowed money and took the plunge. Pope and Swift and Matthew Prior bought stock. Sir Godfrey Kneller, the portrait painter, invested his savings; the poet John Gay, author of *The Beggar's Opera*, was thrilled to be given £2,000 worth of shares by his patron, Mr. Craggs the younger. He was badly in need of money and prudent friends urged him to sell; they argued that an income of £80 a year would at least ensure him " a clean shirt and a leg of mutton every day," but he had visions of a fortune and stubbornly held on.

Why did the South Sea have such magic? Did no one see that the policy of lending money on stock, to buy more stock, must end eventually in disaster? One must remember that the great majority of investors, like those of to-day, knew nothing of finance. It did not occur to them then, any more than to people now, to study a balance sheet before risking their money. They bought on hunch and hearsay. The Government was behind the

South Sea scheme; the King was Governor of the Company:
what could be more solid or respectable?

But what about the bankers and business men? Once the
Company had embarked on its " vicious-circle " policy of loaning out money to keep people buying more stock—which was
done quite openly—did the experts not see that a crash was bound
to come? Wool was pulled over many people's eyes by the fact
that the Bank of England was doing exactly the same thing.
From May until October the Bank lent money on its own stock
with the result that its shares rose from 200 to 265. Mr. Craggs
the younger wrote to Lord Stanhope, who was on a visit to Hanover, " It is impossible to tell you what a rage prevails for South
Sea subscriptions at any price." Mr. Edward Harley wrote to
his brother, Lord Oxford, " The madness of stockjobbing is
inconceivable. The wildness was beyond my thought." And
Lady Molesworth wrote to her husband from Ireland, " I believe
that most of our money is gone over to the South Sea Stock, for
I never saw it so hard to get in my life." If the Bank approved of
South Sea methods, and even copied them, what could be wrong
with them ?

The knowledgeable investors must be divided into two distinct
categories. First came those who were dazzled by the theory of
" credit " and genuinely believed the policy was sound. Credit
was a thrilling new discovery, just as amazing to the people of
the early eighteenth century as atomic energy is to ours. It meant
that fortunes could be built by using the same wealth three and
four times over. The theory was expounded endlessly by Mr.
Law. " Credit well manag'd is worth ten times the amount of
Capital Stock." Writers of the day described it as " the new
alchemy " and the " mine of gold." Undoubtedly a number of
business men, and a few of the South Sea directors, believed that
the Company's credit policy was blazing a new path to prosperity;
and that the circle of selling, lending and buying might be
traversed indefinitely. James Milner, M.P., who bitterly opposed
the scheme, expressed his misgivings to one of the South Sea

directors, and received brief, angry replies which reveal a genuine faith in the undertaking:

May 24, 1720. Sir, I thank you for your advice about the South Sea affair; but am resolved not to sell, nor quit; and am sorry you have had all along so wrong notions, which have not only hurt your self, but some of your friends. I am of opinion our stock will be higher, and remain so; and have no fears on me; though could wish it did not rise so fast.

June 17, 1720. Sir, I am fully convinced many Novembers will pass, before any thing like what you say about my brethren will happen; but your passion, and ungentleman-like language, makes me forbear entering into the dispute, desiring to continue our friendship; so shall I only say, that am more and more sure the South Sea Stock will flourish; and he that does not sell yet, does best.[1]

The second category of knowledgeable investors consisted of the sceptics—and this was by far the larger division. These people regarded the project as a flash in the pan, and knew it would end in ruin. This did not prevent them from speculating in the hope of making quick and easy money. Walpole comes into this group; so does Aislabie, the Duchess of Kendal and even the directors. Some of the doubters took the cynical view that it was a good thing to have the national debt paid off, no matter what the cost to the private individual. " I freely confess," declared a pamphlet writer in March, " that I think it is the Interest of the Kingdom to venture at so bold an undertaking, even though it should give an opportunity to Stockjobbers and publick Robbers, to deceive and over-reach some of the King's unwary and industrious subjects."

This same cynicism was voiced by William King, Archbishop of Dublin in a letter to Lord Molesworth. " I send you the queries about the South Sea, but would not on any account

[1] *The Political State of Great Britain.*

have it known that I am concerned in it, for I think, if the debts of the nation may be paid by the folly of particulars . . . it will be very well for the publick and I know no obligation on me to hinder it. Perhaps what would be spent this way would be spent on gaming or on luxury, and I am of opinion that most that go into the matter are well aware it will not succeed, but hope to sell before the price fall."[1]

A more outspoken speculator was Sarah, Duchess of Marlborough. On May 28th the following news item appeared in the *Daily Post:* " The Duke of Marlborough from £27,000 South Sea stock has made nearly £100,000 but the Duchess drew her money out of the South Sea and put it into the Bank; and on Wednesday her Grace subscribed £2,000 to the Lord Onslow's insurance of ships." The Duke of Marlborough's " withdrawal " was done entirely at Sarah's insistence. At the same time she wrote a blistering letter to a friend. " Every mortal that has common sense or that knows anything of figures sees that 'tis not possible by all the arts and tricks upon earth long to carry £400,000,000 of paper credit with £15,000,000 of specie. This makes me think that this project must burst in a little while and fall to nothing."[2]

These letters, of course, were private. As far as the public was concerned the only shrill warnings in June came from anonymous satirists.

> *A wise man laughed to see an ass*
> *Eat thistles and neglect good grass,*
> *But had the sage beheld the folly*
> *Of late transacted in Change Alley*
> *He might have seen worse asses there*
> *Give solid gold for empty air.*

When Mr. Blunt departed for Tunbridge Wells at the

---

[1] *Joint Stock Companies to 1720:* W R. Scott.
[2] *Marlborough—His Life and Times:* Winston S. Churchill.

beginning of July he was riding high. In the first place he had ceased to be a " mister." The King was so delighted with his £86,000 profit that he rewarded his faithful subject with a baronetcy. Sir John was elated, although this mark of distinction scarcely could have raised his prestige higher than it was. His levees were crowded with the grandest people in the land; he was wined, dined and flattered. " The eyes of the world were turned from the treasury and the chief ministers of state to this great oracle whose word was a law to the Company," declared Mr. Aislabie a year later. " To him we owe every motion and every desperate step . . ."

Sir John was still repeating his maxim about the benefits of raising the price of the stock; and still quoting the Bible. He liked to give the impression that the main purpose of his South Sea scheme was to unite everyone in a glorious combination of riches and brotherly love. He hated party rancour and class divisions. He was the spirit of sweetness and light.

The favours at his disposal—and that of his committee—were two-fold; they could allot subscription shares to their friends, and approve loans. The company's policy of lending money to stock-holders was at the height of its popularity. Although the Board of Directors had stipulated that no single person could borrow more than £5,000 Sir John often turned a blind eye to the regulation. Here are a few of the aristocrats who were favoured, and the sums lent to them: The Duke of Portland, £78,000; Lord Castlemaine, £41,000; Lord Hillsborough, £31,800; Hon. William Chetwynd, £34,000; Marquis of Winchester, £24,500; Lord Rothes, £18,500; Earl of Dunmore, £26,500; Lord Chetwynd, £12,500; Hon. Charles Lumley, £11,000; Duke of Montrose, £13,800; Lord Belhaven, £10,000; Lord Archibald Hamilton, £10,500; Duke of Montagu, £9,000; Lord Fitzwilliam, £8,000; Lord Londonderry, £8,000; Colonel George Churchill, £7,000. However, the man who borrowed most of all is a mystery. His name was John Gumley and he had £97,576.

These names only represent a small number of those who borrowed over the £5,000 ceiling. The pressure for money was obvious; with stocks going up, all that was needed was a loan which could be repaid with the profit. It was easy to see why Sir John and his co-directors were so much in demand. " We have made them Kings," wrote Thomas Brodrick, M.P., to his brother in Ireland, " and they deal with everyone as such."

However, it was not only the upper class that was doing well. With down-payment requirements so small, everyone could have a gamble and plenty of fortunes were made in the lower echelons. An Exchange Alley porter, who immediately became known as " the Duke " made £2,000 and bought himself a splendid carriage. " Our South Sea Equipages increase every day," wrote *Applebee's Journal*, " the City ladies buy South Sea jewels, hire South Sea maids, and take new country South Sea Houses; the gentlemen set up South Sea coaches and buy South Sea estates." Another journalist tried to sum it up more precisely. " We are informed that since the hurly-burly of stock jobbing there has appeared in London 200 new Coaches and Chariots, besides as many more now on the Stocks in the Coach-makers' yards; above 4,000 embroider'd Coats; about 3,000 gold watches at the sides of whores and wives; and some few private acts of charity." The stage lost some of its stars for the *Original Weekly Journal* announced that " Mrs. Barbier, a famous singer at the Playhouse, having gained about £8,000 by South Sea Stock has sung her last Farewell to the stage "; and *Mist's Journal* reported that Counsellor Edwards of the Middle Temple had married another actress—" Madame Brand of Leicester-Fields, a lady of great beauty and fortune having got by the rise of South Sea stock upwards of One Hundred Thousand Pounds." Another lucky speculator was a book-seller by the name of Thomas Guy whose shop was situated at the junction of Lombard Street and Cornhill. He specialised in Bibles and Prayer Books, and decided to chance his earnings on some of the Bubble Companies. He made a fortune, and founded Guy's Hospital.

The coach that took Sir John to Tunbridge Wells was now emblazoned with a coat of arms. " In what splendid equipage he went to the Wells, what respect was paid to him there, with what haughtiness he behaved himself in that place, and how he and his family, when they spoke of the scheme, called it ' Our Scheme ' is not the subject of our discourse," wrote a contemporary historian. " There were witnesses enough of their folly. But certain it is, that he wrote every Post to his Brokers, and no sooner was one parcel of Stock disposed of than he ordered another to be sold." Sir John was selling his stock because he did not see how the South Sea project could be kept afloat longer than November. " One of the South Sea directors going to Tunbridge sent me word he was expecting that time," wrote James Milner, M.P. Most of the other directors, as well, had been prudent enough to realise comfortable gains, which they had invested in land or tucked away in hard cash.

Sir John's immediate problem was how to keep things going at all—even another month. The Company was facing serious difficulties. It had lent so much money that its resources were severely strained. Apart from the £8,500,000 which it had already taken in, it was owed another £60,000,000 by shareholders, due in instalments over a period of time. But it was doubtful whether there was so much loose money in the whole Kingdom. Blunt was certain of one thing. The Bubble Companies, which were absorbing valuable funds, must be curtailed. Certain measures had already been taken against them. Early in June Parliament had passed an Act declaring that companies acting without a charter would be classed as " Public Nuisances," and prosecuted. The King had thrown in his weight by issuing a proclamation, referring to the " unwarrantable practices . . . by ensnaring and defrauding unwary Persons to their utter Impoverishment and Ruin, by taking off the minds of many of our Subjects from attending their lawful Employments, and by introducing a General Neglect of Trade and Commerce . . . and having determined to put the said Act into execution, but being desirous that none of our loving subjects should be ignorant of the same, we have thought fit to issue this our Royal Proclamation."

However, many of the Bubble Companies refused to take notice. They believed they could escape the law by turning themselves into co-partnerships. Consequently the market had been infused by a sort of frenzied vitality. On June 11th, the day of the Proclamation, the *Daily Post* reported, " The hurry of our stock-jobbing bubblers has been so great this week, that it has exceeded all that was ever known. There has been nothing but running about from one coffee-house to another, and from one tavern to another, to subscribe without examining what the proposals were. The general cry has been, ' For G . . .'s sake let us subscribe to something, we don't care what it is ! ' So that, in short, many have taken them at their words, and entered them adventurers in some of the grossest cheats and improbable undertakings that ever the world heard of; and yet by all these the projectors have got money, and have had their subscription full as soon as desired." By the middle of July, however, some of the wilder Bubble Companies had shut up shop; and many petitions for charters had been refused. But the results were not having the required effect. Money was still flowing to the South Sea Company's competitors, this time to the larger and more stable concerns.

Sir John came back to London during the second week in August. On August 4th the South Sea Company had made a second offer to annuitants; and on August 12th it offered a fourth subscription of 10,000 shares to the public. Both operations were successful, but they made the problem of how to direct the available cash to South Sea shares alone, all the more pressing. If the people stopped buying the price would fall.

Sir John realised that somehow the big companies must be attacked. Unfortunately, the two richest, the Royal Exchange and the London Assurance Company, were beyond the grip of the law. They had bought their charters in April for the fancy price of £600,000 which had gone to pay the King's debts.

However, there were four large concerns that might prove vulnerable. Although they were all operating legally their charters dated back many years and it might be possible to prove " non-use " or " mis-use." These were the Royal Lustring, Yorks Buildings, the English Copper Company and the Welsh Copper Company. The latter presented slight difficulties as the Prince of Wales was its Governor. The South Sea directors consulted the Government. They informed the Chancellor of the Exchequer that they were thinking of applying for a writ against the companies. Lord Townshend, who was acting as Regent in the King's absence was also consulted. Both men approved the directors' plan of action and the Lord Justices agreed to grant the order required. Before it was published, however, the judges sent a " compliment " to the Prince of Wales, who was at his Richmond residence, " that the Company of Welch Copper, of which His Royal Highness had been pleased to be chosen Governor, being illegal they were forced to involve it in the said Order; which Compliment His Royal Highness received very graciously, and sent a message to the said Company, desiring them to choose another Governor."

Although the Prince sold stock which gave him a £40,000 profit, his dreams of an even larger fortune were shattered and he was not at all pleased. Lord Townshend wrote to his brother-in-law, Robert Walpole, " The South Sea has sett us upon the Bubbles which we have near demolished. This, I think from my heart, is a right measure for the publick but very ill taken at Richmond."[1]

On the 18th of August the writs were served. When the Lord Justices considered the cases they ruled that, with the exception of the English Copper Company, the concerns were operating illegally. Sir John and his fellow directors had pulled it off; but they had not envisaged the consequences. The stocks of the

[1] *Sir Robert Walpole*: J. H. Plumb.

" out-lawed " companies fell to almost nothing; but so also did the stocks of the respectable giants. Public confidence had been shaken to the marrow; everyone hurried to sell. Within a week Royal Exchange had dropped from 250 to 60, and London Assurance from 175 to 30.

The impact of this wave of selling on South Sea stock was staggering. Both the Government and the directors had over-looked the fact that many speculators had shares in more than one company, and most of them had bought on margin. When the prices fell they were obliged to sell South Sea stock to meet their obligations. On August 17th South Sea stock had stood at 900. On September 28th it was 190. The crash had come with a vengeance.

VI

CRIME AND PUNISHMENT

WHEN Parliament rose at the end of July, Robert Walpole departed for his country house, Houghton, in Norfolk. Every few days he received a letter from his broker, Mr. Jacombe (who was also under-secretary at war), giving him the latest stock market news. Walpole was a heavy speculator. During the past six months he had made large profits from investments in the Royal African Company and the Bank of England, and put his money in land. He had no faith in the South Sea Scheme, but he was deeply impressed by the skill of the directors in manipulating the market. The shares had more than doubled between January and April, and by May 21st had risen to 400. He converted annuities worth £777 a year into South Sea stock; and in June invested about £6,500 for himself and members of his family in the third subscription. He recommended the stock to his friends, on a short term basis, and even tried to persuade the Princess of Wales to speculate in it.

Early in August, Walpole had a letter from Mr. Jacombe which was not assuring. " South Sea is under 900 and all the subscriptions are proportionally fallen . . . We are told that when the present subscription for annuities etc. is over we shall see a great turn in stocks, but I see so many watching to gett out on another rise that I cannot consider they can carry it much longer by any art."[1]

Walpole was not perturbed. His friends in the City told him that a new subscription was in the offing; and the Company always managed to boost the stock with a new issue. He waited until the last ten days of August then instructed Jacombe to sell out

[1] *Sir Robert Walpole*: J. H. Plumb.

the South Sea securities he had bought in June at profit and to invest in the new, fourth subscription which was just being put on the market at £1,000 a share. " To be prepared to invest heavily, and to encourage others to invest in the South Sea Company as late as 24th August, 1720, showed either a thirst for a gamble or a lack of common sense or both—at least when conducted from Norfolk," declares Walpole's latest biographer.[1] But this judgement does not take into account the prevailing opinion of the day. The directors had impressed everybody with their market manœuvres. Even the most confirmed sceptics, who cried continuously that the Company would end in ruin, were astonished by the suddenness of the collapse—and the fact that it came when it did. " I owne," wrote Thomas Brodrick, M.P., to his brother on September 13th, " I thought they would carry on the cheat somewhat longer. Various are the conjectures why they suffered the cloud to break soe early, I made no doubt butt 'twould doe soe when they found it to their advantage, which nott being the case at this time, some other reason must bee found . . .[2]" Another M.P., Mr. James Milner, expressed the same view in a letter on the 28th. " I said, indeed, that ruin must soon come upon us, but I own it came two months sooner than I expected. I often said November would be the month."[2]

Despite his unfortunate decision, Walpole was spared by a stroke of luck. Jacombe was unable to buy, privately, any of the fourth issue, as the directors wanted to make " a crowd at the books "; so he did not buy at all. However, far from realising a profit on Walpole's third subscription shares he got rid of them at a loss. The price had begun to drop, and Jacombe held on a few days waiting for a rise. Up till now the directors had always managed to inspire a wave of buying with every new issue. This time the rise never came. As we know, the writ of August 18th had sent all stocks tumbling down, and people had to find cash

---

[1] *Sir Robert Walpole:* J. H. Plumb.
[2] *Parliamentary History.*

to meet their obligations. On September 1st South Sea stock was 770; on the 9th it was 575; and on the 19th, 380.[1]

Meanwhile the directors were playing every card—and even cards they did not possess—to prevent a collapse. On August 30th they made the astonishing announcement that the Company would pay a 30% dividend at Christmas, and after that an annual dividend of 50% for the next twelve years. This kept the stock at 800 for a few days, but the pressure for ready cash was too great and selling began again. On September 8th a stockholders' meeting was held at the Merchant Tailors' Hall at nine in the morning. The object was to calm the investors and persuade them not to sell. James Craggs, the elder, spoke for the Government urging " calmness and union " and praising the directors for their " skilful and prudent management." Mr. Hungerford, M.P., flung reserve to the winds and declared that no one had " ever performed such wonderful things in so short a time, as the South Sea managers had brought about." He made the astonishing declaration that " they had done more than the Crown, the pulpit, and the magistrate could do: for they had reconciled all parties in one common interest, and thereby laid asleep, if not wholly extinguished, domestic jars and animosities: that by the rise of their stocks the monied-men had vastly increased their fortunes: the country gentlemen had seen the value of their lands doubled and trebled in their hands; and they had, at the same time, done good to the Church, not a few of the reverend clergy having got great sums by this project: that, in short, they had inriched the whole nation; and he hoped they had not forgot themselves."[2] The Duke of Portland wound up the

---

[1] On September 6th Jacombe drew up a statement of Walpole's account with his firm. Having got rid of his third subscription shares Walpole's only South Sea holdings on that date were those he had received from the conversion of his annuities; these consisted of about 54 shares which had been acquired at £375 each. Since South Sea stock did not fall below 570 until September 10th, and not below 400 until September 19th, he undoubtedly sold them at a profit.

[2] *Parliamentary History.*

proceedings with the crisp observation that "he did not know what reasons anybody had to be dissatisfied." He discovered a few reasons a fortnight later when he learned that most of his fortune had melted away.

By the following week South Sea stock had fallen to 380. The directors were so desperate they decided to swallow their pride and appeal to the Bank of England for assistance. James Craggs arranged a meeting between the two companies at his house on the 19th. He invited Walpole, who was in London tending to his personal affairs, and begged him to persuade the Bank to help. Five directors from each side were present; among them were Sir Gilbert Heathcote and Mr. Nathaniel Gould of the Bank, and Sir John Fellows and Sir Charles Joye of the Company. The discussion lasted several hours and was fairly sticky, for the Bank had no wish to get mixed up in the mess. In the end, however, the bankers bowed to the pleas and agreed to circulate three and a half million pounds of South Sea bonds which they would purchase at £400 each. Robert Walpole undoubtedly played a major part in wringing this commitment from them as he was asked to put the understanding in writing. He scribbled a draft, which still exists, and is known as "the Bank contract."

Although the agreement looked feasible on the 19th, it appeared in a very different light on the 24th. On that day the South Sea Company's bankers, the Sword Blade Company, ran out of specie, and shut up shop. This increased the panic and the stock fell to 190. The Bank of England's promise to buy shares at 400 looked pretty foolish, and its managers hastily searched for a way out. They conveniently came to the conclusion that their contract was not legal without the sanction of Parliament, and wrote a polite letter saying that the deal was off.

This behaviour was more practical than ethical. However, the Bank was finding it difficult to maintain its own credit. Everyone who could, was selling something and demanding specie. Walpole was among them. He collected a large bag of gold, and departed for Houghton. By this time the Bank was forced to employ certain ruses in order to meet the run upon it. "It employed a number of clerks to tell out the money which was demanded, as well as what was brought in. Payments were made in light sixpences and shillings, and large sums were paid to particular friends, who went out with their bags at one door, to deliver them to people placed at another, who were let in to pay the same money to tellers, who took time to count it over. These persons were, of course, always served first. By this means time was gained, the friends of the Bank rallied round it, and made large subscriptions to support the company."[1] Among the Bank's "friends" were the Prince of Wales who, with a great flourish, paid in £50,000; and the King, who sent a message from Hanover instructing his Lord Commissioners of the Treasury to deposit £100,000 on his behalf.

Meanwhile the country was in an uproar. "All is floating," wrote Matthew Prior, "all falling; the directors are curst; the top adventurers broke, four goldsmiths walked off, Walpole and Townshend sent for that they may settle matters, *sed adhuc sine successu*, and every man with a face as long as Godolphin's; *vogue la galère*, I must fare like the rest."

The propertied class was hit almost to the last family, simply because its members had found it easy to raise money for speculation on their mortgages. The Duke of Chandos had lost the £300,000 he had amassed as Paymaster of the Forces. "All he gained by fraud, he lost by stocks," jibed Swift. He possessed such vast estates he managed to keep going throughout his lifetime on credit alone; but when he died, Cannons, the huge house he had built for £200,000, was pulled down and the materials sold to pay off his debts. The Duke of Portland was in an even worse way; he had lost so much money he had to leave England. He applied to the King for a colonial governorship and was given Jamaica. He set sail at the end of 1721 and remained there until his death four years later. Lord Irwin and Lord Lonsdale followed

---

[1] *History of the Bank of England*: A. Andréades.

suit. They were obliged to accept such primitive posts as the Leeward Islands and the Barbados, but they considered themselves lucky to have a refuge of any kind.

The Dukes of Bolton[1] and Wharton managed to stay in England but their scale of living was drastically impaired and Lord Londonderry bored everyone by bemoaning the loss of £50,000. " Weekly through the streets of London," lamented *Applebee's Journal* on October 22nd, " you may see second-hand coaches; second-hand gold watches, cast-off diamond watches and earrings to be sold; servants already want places who were, but a little while ago, so saucy and insolent, no wages and no kind of usage cou'd oblige them; Long Lane, Monmouth and Regent Fair are full of rich liveries to be sold, nay, and full of rich embroider'd petticoats, rich, embroider'd coats and waistcoats; in a word every place is full of the ruin of Exchange Alley . . ."

The gentry was hit even harder than the aristocracy because of lesser resources upon which to raise credit. Properties were put up for sale, gentlemen searched for work, and squires' daughters took jobs with the *nouveaux riches* as governesses. A Norfolk land-owner, Colonel Windham, wrote to his brother on September 27th, " There never was such distraction and undoing in any country. You can't suppose the number of familys undone. One may almost say every body is ruin'd, who has traded beyond their Stock. Many a £100,000 man not worth a groat; and it grieves me to think of some of them . . . They call South Sea 300, but there are no buyers. Mr. Walpole and ye Managers give us hopes of better things in a few days. Not a penny stirring."[2]

The intellectuals lost most of their savings. Their only recourse was more work. Sir Godfrey Kneller, the portrait painter,

---

[1] Bolton was described by a contemporary as " a most lewd, vicious man, a great dissembler and a heavy drinker." Despite his South Sea losses he was able to keep afloat, in every sense; in November he managed to secure a pension from the Government for £3,000 a year in recognition of past services as Lord Lieutenant of Ireland.

[2] *Norfolk Portraits*: R. W. Ketton-Cremer, Faber.

had entertained visions of a leisurely old age, now he had to look again for commissions. Samuel Chandler, a famous non-conformist minister, was compelled to try and eke out a living by opening a bookshop. Alexander Pope and Matthew Prior suffered heavily. John Gay, the poet, whose friends had begged him to sell out when his stocks were worth £20,000 was destitute; he took his loss so hard he retired to his bed and nearly died of a broken heart. Alexander Pope, on the other hand, could afford to be more philosophical as he still retained something. " Methinks God has punished the avaritious," he wrote to Bishop Atterbury, " as he often punishes sinners, in their own way, in the very sin itself; the thirst for gain was their crime, that thirst continued became their punishment and ruin. As for the very few who have the good fortune to remain with half of what they imagined they had (among whom is your humble servant) I would have them sensible of their felicity, and convinced of the truth of old Hesiod's maxim, who after half his estate was swallowed up by the directors of those days, resolved that half to be more than the whole."[1]

Every day the chaos grew worse. " 'Tis almost unfashionable not to be a bankrupt," cried a public speaker at a meeting on September 30th. " The Credit of our nation . . . that has stood the shock of so many wars . . . is at present on the very brink of destruction. Every transfer day brings on the ruin of a hundred families, and there is scarce a gentleman who hears me, but has felt the dismal effects of what has lately happened, either in himself, his relations or his friends." Even those who had not speculated were feeling the pinch. Shopkeepers and proprietors were unable to sell their goods or collect their bills. Every morn-ing the papers announced that more goldsmiths and brokers had put up notices and skipped abroad. If they remained in England they would land in a debtors' prison. So frequent was this recourse, that a cartoon was published depicting a foreign coffee house crowded with refugees. The proprietor is saying: " You

[1] Pope's *Letters*.

must lie four in a bed and 'twill be impossible to find room for all the Merchants I expect here this night."

The *London Gazette* was filled with bankruptcy notices but some preferred " to take a swing out of the world by way of relief to their vexations "—as one flippant journalist put it. Suicides became so commonplace, scarcely a day passed without a notice, tucked into the miscellaneous column of the newspapers, of a gentleman who had drowned himself, a stockjobber who had cut his throat from ear to ear, or a merchant who had blown out his brains. " Last week a gentleman hanged himself at his house by Golden Square," reported the *Weekly Journal* on October 29th, " his servant coming accidentally into the room, and seeing his master in that condition, was very much surprised; but however had courage enough to cut him down before he was quite dead, tho' to very little purpose, for the next day the poor gentleman departed this life; 'tis reported of him, that having shelter'd himself from his creditors for some time in the Mint, as soon as the opportunity of retrieving a broken fortune presented itself in Change Alley, he became an Adventurer with such success as enabled him to pay his debts, which he did very thoroughly; but presuming he had enough left him to afford a handsome maintenance for the future, upon the fall of the stocks grew so melancholy; and his dejection of spirit prevailed so much on him, as to hurry him on to this unnatural remedy. The Coroner's Inquest have sat on the Body, and brought in their verdict NON COMPOS MENTIS."

Meanwhile rage against the South Sea directors was mounting daily. One of the most curious aspects of the South Sea crash was that no one, not even the financial experts, ascribed the sudden fall to its proximate cause—the writ of August 18th. Accusations spread like wild-fire that the collapse was due to the dishonesty of the directors; some put it down to their greed in raising the third and fourth subscriptions to £1,000, others to heavy and secret selling of their own holdings for exorbitant profits. All this was true, but it still was not the main cause of the disaster.

Even if the scheme had been honestly administered, it could not have succeeded.

The public was in no mood to be meticulous. It was determined to have revenge and every fresh allegation against the directors added grist to its mill. At a South Sea meeting on September 30th, one of the stockholders, Captain Maggot, declared that he knew of a director who had sold above £50,000 of the third subscription at two hundred and thirty per cent. premium. Another stockholder, Mr. Walker, called for an enquiry. It was the same to him, he said, whether he was plundered by a cabal of sharpers and their adherents in a committee, or by a troop of horse at Newmarket. He insisted on retribution, and proposed setting up a committee " to bring to justice the betrayers of their country." A Mr. Bludgel rose and scotched the committee idea, declaring that the fall in stock was entirely due to " malicious rumours."

There was no stopping these rumours. The truth was that they had started circulating long ago, when the South Sea Bill was first passed. Everyone knew of the directors' " sharp practices " but no one minded when the stock was rising. Colonel Windham reflected the opinion of the country in a letter to his brother on November 25th. " We are here in a most sad state between Hope and Despair. Allmost everyone gives great Assurances. Mr. Walpole is said often to declare he thinks his scheme will do, but ye Parliament is put off, and people are frighten'd, and so stock falls ... Allmost all one knows or sees are upon ye very Brink of Destruction, and those who were reckon'd to have done well yesterday are found stark nought to day. Those Devills of Directors have ruin'd more men's fortunes in this world than I hope old Beelzebub will do souls for ye next ... If ye Ministry do nothing after all their promises, they are as bad as ye Directors."[1]

The country waited impatiently for the recall of Parliament.

[1] *Norfolk Portraits:* R. W. Ketton-Cremer.

But a new session could not be opened without the King, and the King was still in Hanover. He had left England in June and had not planned to return until the first of December. Lord Sunderland was with him, and every post brought the British minister distraught, hysterical reports on the state of the nation. " Upon the first news we had of the unhappy turn the Stocks and publick Credit had taken," Sunderland wrote to Lord Carlisle on October 19th, " we got the King to fix the meeting of Parliament for the 25th of November. Since then, within these three or four days, we have had the news of the Credit's being lower and lower, and of things being every day in a worse condition, the King had taken the resolution of going over so as to hold the Parliament on the 8th of November, which is as soon as it is possible for him to be there, and orders are sent for the necessary notice. I myself should have set out as soon as we had the news of this melancholy state of things, which was but three or four days ago, but that I thought the first necessary step was to fix the King's going as soon as possible, and now that is done, I shall set out from this place to-morrow, so that I hope in a very few days to have the honour of kissing your hands in England."[1]

In the end, however, the King did not return to London until November 12th, and Parliament was not opened until December 8th. It was thought best to allow time for passions to subside. The Government hoped that by some miracle the royal presence would restore confidence, but on the day of George's landing at Margate, South Sea stock fell from 210 to 135. The Sovereign's Hanoverian advisors were appalled by the heavily charged atmosphere that greeted them. They discovered that the King was accused of conniving with the South Sea directors, that his name was being bandied about the coffee houses as one of the architects of the disaster. Some were so worried they suggested sending for German soldiers who could be relied upon to maintain order in case a revolt broke out; others hinted that it might be necessary for him to abdicate in favour of his son. Fortunately

[1] *The First George*: Lewis Melville.

for George, the British ministers presented a more stolid front, and no hasty acts were thrust upon him.

Meanwhile, Robert Walpole had been giving much thought to the role he was to play in the new session. He was not smeared with the South Sea brush; he had argued in favour of the Bank when the proposals were before Parliament; and he had strongly supported the key motion which, if passed, would have reduced the South Sea Company's opportunity to speculate. He loathed Sunderland and mistrusted Stanhope, and would not be sorry to see them both discredited. All this pointed to the likelihood that he might sit back and let the Government flounder in its own mud. But Walpole was not as stupid as that. He wanted power. He was a Whig and if the Whig Government fell, he probably would fall with it. Furthermore, all authority stemmed from the King, and he was not likely to incur George's gratitude by refusing to try and shelter his ministers and favourites from the blast of public disapproval. Lastly the King was Governor of the South Sea Company; the less dishonourable its proceedings appeared, the better for the monarch's good name.

Walpole's course was clear. He would defend ministers, favourites, and directors with every resource and artifice at his command. He would concentrate on a remedy. It would not be easy, for whatever arrangements were made, the public would have to understand that there was no legal escape from their losses; and that South Sea contracts must be honoured. However, Walpole's friend and adviser, Mr. Robert Jacombe, had suggested that the Bank and the East India Company might be persuaded to take over a large proportion of the debt which the South Sea Company had converted; this would go some way to relieve the plight of the investors. Thus resolved and fortified, Walpole marched into one of the stormiest battles Parliament has ever known.

The House was flooded with petitions from all parts of the country calling on the Government to punish the authors of the calamity—and making it clear that the authors were none other than the South Sea directors. The King's speech was carefully designed to lower the temperature. It stressed the flourishing state of the nation's foreign trade. This was perfectly true. Although the stock market had upset the internal credit, business abroad went on as usual, and was in a remarkably healthy way. He then bade the House to summon all its "prudence, temper and resolution to find out and apply the proper remedies to our misfortunes."

But it was clear from the beginning that the House was in no mood to concern itself merely with remedies. It was in an ugly, vindictive frame of mind. Members had convinced themselves, like the country as a whole, that the South Sea scheme had been ruined by the greed and dishonesty of the directors. They conveniently overlooked the fact that they, the members of Parliament, had passed a Bill that was unworkable. The only way the Company could raise the £7,500,000 it had promised to pay the Government was to inflate the stock way above its true value. This had been emphasised time and again by the scheme's opponents. We know that the leading ministers pushed the Bill through because they received free gifts of stocks; that many M.P.s supported it for the same reason; that other M.P.s gave their assent because they saw an opportunity to make easy money by speculation. No doubt there were members who genuinely believed in the Bill, but the majority had reservations which were overcome by the argument that it was better to try and solve the debt problem than not try at all—and the desire for private gain. Over 450 members of both Houses had gambled in the stock, and many had not hesitated to accept preferential terms from the directors. Their deep anger was cloaked by moral platitudes: but it sprang from the fact that instead of making money they had lost it.

Chagrin compelled them to find a scapegoat. The mal-practices of the directors (which many of them had been aware of from the beginning) offered a heaven sent excuse. It allowed them to ease their consciences and vent their rage. Smarting under heavy financial losses, and soon genuinely convinced of the righteousness of their cause, they were ready to tear the directors to pieces. Lord Molesworth, a fiery Anglo-Irish radical, made this plain when he replied to the King's speech. Before members looked for " remedies," he said, they ought to enquire into " the cause and nature of the distemper "; like surgeons, they ought to cut out " the venomous core " of the wound before applying a healing plaster. " He owned that it had been by some suggested, that there was no law to punish the Directors of the South Sea Company, who were justly looked upon as the immediate authors of the present misfortunes: but that, in his opinion, they ought, on this occasion, to follow the example of the ancient Romans, who having no law against parricide, because their legislators supposed no son could be so unnaturally wicked, as to embrue his hands in his father's blood, made one to punish so heinous a crime, as soon as it happened to be committed; and adjudged the guilty wretch to be thrown alive, sewed up in a sack, into the Tyber. Concluding, That as he looked upon the contrivers and executers of the villainous South Sea Scheme, as the parricides of their country, he should be satisfied to see them undergo the same punishment."[1] Sir Joseph Jekyll then leapt up and backed Molesworth to the hilt. Where the laws were deficient " the legislative authority may and ought to exert itself."

Walpole saw that it was going to be even more difficult than he had imagined. Because of his huge bulk he often was alluded to as " the great man." As he stood, surveying the House, he was an impressive sight; but no one much liked the note he struck. He had never approved of the South Sea scheme, he said, and was sensible that it had done a great deal of mischief. " But since it could not be undone he thought it the duty of all good men to give their helping hand toward retrieving it; and that with this in view he had already bestowed some thoughts on a proposal

[1] *Parliamentary History.*

to restore public credit, which at a proper time he would submit to the House."[1]

For the next ten days the debate followed a set pattern. Infuriated M.P.s called again and again for punitive action, while Walpole cleverly fended them off with earnest evasions. His line was always the same. He reminded them repeatedly of " the bleeding condition " of the national credit and insisted that the only thing that mattered was a solution. He warned the House that if they continued " in a warm passionate way " the scheme he was working on might be " rendered impracticable." " He desired that the House would proceed regularly and calmly lest by running precipitately into odious enquiries, they should exasperate the distemper to such a degree as to render all remedies ineffectual."[1]

The Opposition saw through Walpole's game, and more than one speaker bitterly accused him of " screening " the culprits. This description seemed peculiarly apt in view of his twenty-stone figure, and soon all his enemies were referring to him as " the Skreen " or " The Skreen-master General." Nevertheless his tactics were successful. By the Christmas recess the only thing the Opposition had achieved was to compel the South Sea directors to lay their books and proceedings before the House. This was done on December 15th. On the 21st Walpole presented his proposals for restoring the credit. They consisted of engrafting £9,000,000 of South Sea stock into the Bank of England and a like amount into the East India Company. The scheme was not compulsory, and the House invited the two companies named to come forward with proposals. Then it rose for Christmas.

For a brief moment it looked as though Walpole's manœuvres might succeed in keeping the hounds permanently at bay. South Sea stock rose from 135 to 210 on the strength of his proposition, and the House met again on January 4th in a far more equable mood. The spell did not last long. The Govern-

[1] *Parliamentary History.*

ment, perhaps guided by Walpole, made the mistake of introducing the annual Mutiny Bill. This was such a transparent move
to delay the debate on " the public credit " that it stung the
Opposition to fury. Never, cried Sir Joseph Jekyll, had the Bill
been brought in so early in the session. Clearly such a hurry was
intended " to stop the prosecution of the authors of the present
misfortunes." They all very well knew, he continued, that the
days of members were numbered, and that as soon as they had
dispatched the money Bills and the Bill now moved for, they
should immediately be dispatched home: that therefore he was
for staying those Bills, until they had done justice to the nation,
who called aloud for it. Mr. Craggs, the younger, replied smugly
that he was surprised to see such opposition to a Bill so necessary
for the safety of the Government. Lord Molesworth then rose
and said " Mr. Speaker, Is it come to this, that every man who
has a place must do all the drudgery that is enjoined him ? " Sir
Joseph Jekyll intervened again and said that he was as zealous as
any man for the service of the King and his government, but he
believed that punishing those who had brought the nation into
the present calamitous condition was the most effective way to
serve the King . . .[1]

In the end the Mutiny Bill was brought forward and examined
by the House in a sullen mood. As soon as it was dealt with, the
Opposition returned to the attack with more spleen and determination than ever before. Now things began to move fast.
Jekyll moved that the thirty-three directors and officers of the
South Sea Company be restrained from leaving the Kingdom
for one year. The motion was carried by a large majority. Mr.
Shippen, an ardent Jacobite, who hated Hanoverians and Whigs
with equal intensity, expressed his pleasure, then looked straight
at Mr. Craggs and declared that there were some men in great
stations, no less guilty than the directors, whom in time, he would
not hesitate to name. Mr. Craggs lost his head and declared that
he was ready to give satisfaction to any man, either in the House

[1] *Parliamentary History.*

or out of it. " This expression gave no small offence; and thereupon the Lord Molesworth replied that he had the honour to be a member of that House upwards of thirty years, and never before now knew any man bold enough to challenge the whole House of Commons, and all England besides: that for his part, though past sixty, he would answer whatever Mr. Craggs had to say within the House, and hoped there were young members enough, that would not be afraid to look him in the face out of the House. Upon this, Mr. Craggs seeing the House in a great ferment, got up again, and said, that by giving satisfaction, he meant clearing his conduct."[1]

The Opposition members had the bit in their teeth and Walpole saw that there was no stopping them. They voted to set up a Secret Committee composed of thirteen members to be selected by ballot. Their task would be to examine the " books, papers and persons " of the directors and anyone else connected with the South Sea project. The House chose the most violent and intractable opponents of the Company to serve on the Committee. Mr. Thomas Brodrick was elected chairman, and among his assistants were old Governor Pitt (who had sold his diamond to the Regent), Lord Molesworth, Sir Joseph Jekyll, General Ross, a choleric, unforgiving martinet, and Mr. Archibald Hutcheson, the economist who had written so many virulent pamphlets against the South Sea Bill. The Committee lost no time in setting about their task. They began calling witnesses at once, and worked six days a week from nine in the morning until eleven at night.

The Lords refused to be outdone. They viewed the Commons with a jealous eye, and a few days later announced that they would open an enquiry of their own. All directors and officers of the South Sea Company, who were not members of the Commons, would be summoned the following week to give evidence. Needless to say this decision resulted in considerable confusion with directors scurrying back and forwards between the two

[1] *Parliamentary History.*

chambers, the books and papers wanted in one place, always in another.

This was not all. The Commons introduced a Bill restraining the directors from leaving the Kingdom, demanding £25,000 bail each, and instructing them to submit an inventory of the full amount of their property " reall and personall." The directors petitioned both chambers for the right to be heard by counsel, but their request was indignantly rejected. Several M.P.s braved the wrath of the House by insisting that it was the right of every individual to be heard in his own defence; but their colleagues replied that the directors' papers and accounts already showed them guilty of a notorious breach of trust. " The case was no more or other than committing or requiring bail from a criminal upon confession," wrote Thomas Brodrick, explaining the mood of the House. " From the notoriety of the thing . . . the legislature were now doing what in ordinary cases the magistrate might and ought to doe."[1]

Not everyone agreed with this interpretation. Years later, Edward Gibbon, the great historian, and a grandson of one of the directors, dealt with Parliament's high-handed action in sweeping terms. " A Bill of pains and penalties was introduced, a retroactive statute, to punish the offenses, which did not exist at the time they were committed. Such a pernicious violation of liberty and law can be excused only by the most imperious necessity; nor could it be defended on this occasion by the plea of impending danger or useful example. The legislature restrained the persons of the Directors, imposed an exorbitant security for their appearance, and marked their characters with a previous note of ignominy; they were compelled to deliver, upon oath, the strict value of their estates; and were disabled from making any transfer or alienation of any part of their property. Against a bill of pains and penalties it is the common right of every subject to be heard by his counsel at the bar; they prayed to be heard; their prayer was refused; and their

[1] *Parliamentary History.*

oppressors, who required no evidence, would listen to no defence."[1]

Our old acquaintance, Sir John Blunt, now appears on the scene again. There is very little mention of this gentleman from the time we left him, in the middle of August, pressing for writs to be served against the South Sea Company's four big rivals, until the month of January, 1721, when the Secret Committee demanded his presence. He is named as attending one or two directors' meetings in the autumn, but played no major part. An anonymous contemporary reporter declares that he was furious to be called back to London from Tunbridge Wells in August, when things were getting sticky. "He used the sub-Governor in a very rough manner, saying amongst other things: that he did not know but it might have cost him his life to have left off drinking the waters so abruptly; and that he had rather given £10,000 than to have come up to town."[1]

Perhaps Sir John decided that since the game was up, it was best to retire permanently to the soothing waters of Tunbridge Wells. He had no personal worries, as his money was safely secured in land and gold. However, as soon as the Secret Committee started its enquiry, several directors made it clear that Blunt was the "contriver" of the South Sea scheme and he was summoned without more ado. He was not a satisfactory witness. Whatever question he was asked, he simply replied that he could not remember. The cashier, Mr. Knight, found it more difficult to evade his interrogators. He had taken care to present the least damaging of his account books, had torn out pages and rubbed out names. Nevertheless, it was not easy to invent alibis. Sir John conferred daily with Knight, Sir Charles Joye and Sir John Fellows in an attempt to make their answers tally. Mr. Knight had carried out most of the transactions—by instruction, of course; if no one volunteered the information, it would be impossible for the Secret Committee to determine who had

[1] *Memoirs*: Edward Gibbon.

given those instructions. Knight, however, was bordering on a nervous breakdown. If he were forced to reveal everything, he declared, " there would be a scene such as the world had never before witnessed." The best solution was for him to disappear.

What country could he flee to, and remain safe from the long arm of the British Parliament? No one knows exactly what happened, but circumstances suggest that Sir John conferred with Craggs the younger, who was still second in command of foreign affairs, and perhaps Craggs consulted the Duchess of Kendal. On January 23rd, two days before the bill restraining South Sea officers from leaving the Kingdom became law, the House was informed that Mr. Knight had skipped abroad, embarking at Dover and landing at Calais. He had written a farewell letter to the South Sea directors. " Self-preservation has compelled me to withdraw myself," he explained. He went on to add that he had taken a little of the Company's money " sufficient to maintain myself." This was an understatement as he had helped himself to a very large sum; indeed at this precise moment he was sailing on a specially chartered yacht in the direction of the Low Countries, not wishing to risk capture by travelling overland.

The House received the news in a fury of excitement. They appealed to the King to stop the ports and offer a reward for his capture. His Majesty obliged and the sum of £2,000 was put on Knight's head. At the same time Lord Townshend, President of the Council, announced that messengers had been dispatched to twelve of His Majesty's ministers abroad, asking for their help in detaining the culprit. These acts met with success. On February 9th Townshend informed a delighted House that Knight had been arrested by a posse of soldiers in an inn at Tirlemont on his way from Brussels to Liége. These cities and a considerable piece of territory around them constituted the " Brabant States," which in turn formed part of the Austrian Netherlands. The province was ruled from Vienna by England's faithful friend, the Emperor Charles. The bird was nearly in hand; but not quite.

Craggs, Senior (above, left) Craggs, Junior (above, right), Stanhope (below). Stanhope was expected to defend his colleagues, the Craggses, both of whom were deeply implicated in the South Sea scandal; but all three died suddenly before justice could take its course

The Netherland Governor, the Marquis de Prie, was asked to surrender Knight to the British authorities, but a month passed and nothing happened. On March 20th an astonishing letter was read to the House of Commons. It came from Mr. Leathes, the British Resident in Brussels. Although Leathes " had made the most pressing instances with the Marquis de Prie for the delivering up of Knight " the Governor regretted that he could not comply unless the Emperor instructed him to do so; and the Emperor's decision was likely to be in the negative because of the peculiar rights enjoyed by the Brabant States. Apparently, continued Mr. Leathes, the Brabant Secretary had called upon the Marquis twice to remind him " that according to one of the articles of the joyful entry of Brabant, which was granted them by the Emperor Charles V, and has been sworn to by all his successors, and which they look upon as their Magna Carta, no person charged with, or apprehended for any crime, can be removed or tried out of their province."[1] The relevant article then was read out and M.P.s learned that it stemmed back to the year 1354 when the Duke of Brabant, who had no heir, asked that his son-in-law should succeed him. In order to persuade his subjects to accept a change of dynasty he promised them for all time, immunity from extradition.

It did not take the House long to realise that it was being diddled. It was inconceivable that the Emperor of Austria would refuse the King of England a favour over a matter of no concern either to himself or the Brabanters. Obviously the whole thing was pre-arranged, probably by George himself, through pressure from the Duchess of Kendal. Lord Molesworth stormed with indignation. He did not dare to make a treasonable attack on his sovereign but he branded the Emperor's excuse for refusing to help as " a frivolous pretense " and suggested revising the Austrian treaty. It would be good to know, he thundered, " upon what motives we have been at so great an expense of blood and treasure, and have sent our men-of-war to rot and be

[1] *Parliamentary History.*

worm-eaten in the Mediterranean, to conquer Kingdoms for the Emperor."

Despite all the clamour and fulminating, Mr. Knight remained at large. A cartoon was published showing the Duchess of Kendal slipping him a bag of gold and entitled "The Brabant Screen." This lady's role became more obvious a year later when a Knight suddenly turned up in Paris. She informed the Regent that, despite the British Ambassador's request for Knight's extradition, the King would rather he remained abroad. And so the matter rested. Knight lived a comfortable and agreeable life in Paris on his ill-gotten gains, and even managed to build up another fortune.

While this was going on, Parliament had not been idle. Members were so enraged and shocked by the initial news of Knight's disappearance that they took a number of hasty and high-handed actions. The Commons summoned the four M.P.s who were also South Sea directors—Sir Theodore Janssen, Sir Robert Chaplin, Mr. Sawbridge and Mr. Eyles—then ordered the door of the chamber locked and the keys placed upon the table. General Ross declared that they had discovered "a train of the deepest villainy and fraud that Hell ever contrived to ruin a nation," recommended searching the directors' houses and seizing their books and papers, and taking action to make sure that no others escaped. The four M.P.s were expelled from the House and taken into custody; Mr. Aislabie resigned his post; the directors were forbidden to serve on the board of any major company, and those who held positions under the Crown were dismissed. This last order concerned Mr. Edmondson, purser to the *Royal Anne*, the Navy's prize man-of-war; Mr. Hawes, Receiver-General of Customs; Sir Harcourt Master, Receiver-General of the City of London; Mr. Reynolds, Commissioner of the Victualling Office; Mr. Houlditch of the Stamp Office; and Mr. Ingram of the Duty on Salt. Again, not to be outdone, the

Lords ordered Black Rod to take five directors, whom they were questioning, into custody. They were Sir William Chapman, Mr. Chester, Mr. Gibbon, Mr. Hawes and Mr. Houlditch.

The Secret Committee set to work once more, this time without the assistance of Knight. They found his absence a severe handicap. The directors now were able to say that he had concluded transactions without their knowledge or concurrence; and with no reminders to prompt them, they were unable to recall facts. After a few days, it was clear that the Committee was getting nowhere. Something had to be done. Every man had his price, so Sir Joseph Jekyll and Lord Molesworth approached Sir John Blunt and asked for his help. If he would give them a " lead," they promised to see that his case was treated with leniency.

Sir John was always ready to strike a bargain. The rage against the directors was mounting each day. Their estates were already virtually confiscated by the Government—it only remained for Parliament to decide whether any part of them would be remitted to their owners. Sir John was prepared to save what he could, and agreed to the proposal. That evening, when Sir Charles Joye called upon him, as usual, to ask what had been said in the morning interrogation, he was astonished by the change he found. Sir John said that he had come to the conclusion that it was best to tell the whole truth. " What," cried Sir Charles, " about the ladies and all?" " Yes," replied Sir John. " The examination is very strict and nothing but the truth will do."[1]

Sir John told the Committee that Mr. Knight kept two books —one was a " green Book " which he had taken abroad with him and which contained the transactions of a more personal nature. About a million and a quarter pounds had been spent on bribes but he could not recall all the recipients. The ones that came to mind were the Duchess of Kendal, £10,000; Madame Kielmansegge, £10,000; the latter's two nieces, £10,000;

[1] *Parliamentary History.*

Lord Sunderland, £50,000; Craggs the elder, £30,000; and Mr. Charles Stanhope, £10,000.

Blunt made it clear that the payments to the ladies were made at the insistence of Craggs the younger, who named the price that would be considered " agreeable." Blunt told how he waited upon the Duchess, accompanied by Sir John Fellows, the sub-Governor, " and aquainted her with the proposals." It was delicately put. She was told that the Company desired her " good offices " in return for which Mr. Knight would " follow her directions." Madame Kielmansegge did not receive such V.I.P. treatment. Blunt and Fellows merely wrote her a joint letter making an offer, which she accepted.

At last the Committee had something to put its teeth into. The directors were interrogated along the course Sir John had opened up and a good deal of corroboration was obtained. The House of Lords, in the meantime, had stumbled on the fact that Mr. Aislabie possessed an account with a brokerage firm (in the name of his son-in-law Mr. Wallace), showing a balance of £794,000.

The findings began to leak out long before the reports were published, and London drawing-rooms buzzed with the gossip that five ministers—Sunderland, Aislabie, Mr. Charles Stanhope and the two Craggs—were deeply implicated in the scandal. There were six reports in all and the first two were laid before the House in the last half of February. They came almost as an anti-climax. The main point was the bribery, and names and sums were given. However, it was clear that many hundreds of thousands of pounds spent for this purpose were still untraced, and probably would remain so unless Knight was brought back to England. A number of M.P.s undoubtedly drew deep breaths of relief. The reports went on to list dozens of malpractices; the ministers as well as directors, had been allowed to allocate huge blocks of shares to their friends; more stock had been issued than legally authorised; the Company several times had bought its own stock to keep up the quotations—and on these occasions

directors frequently sold their private stock to the Company for
the highest possible prices. The chicanery was endless. The
Company's brokerage firms, as well as its bankers, the Sword
Blade Company, were all involved in a net-work of manipulation. The House listened tirelessly to the long complicated
allegations, then passed ten resolutions naming the directors
guilty of a gross breach of trust. They would be punished in due
course; but first, members insisted, the case of the ministers must
be considered.

The Government braced itself for the attack. It was in a
particularly groggy condition, due to the fact that two weeks
earlier it had suffered a smashing blow by the sudden death of
Earl Stanhope. This incorruptible lord was the only leading
minister whose reputation was entirely unsmirched by the South
Sea scandal. All Whig hopes were centred upon him as the example that might save the Ministry. The circumstances of his
death were odd. He had attended a debate in the House of Lords
on February 4th. The peers were in a bad mood because Sir John
Blunt, who had been summoned before them, refused to answer
their questions. He had given evidence in " the other place," and
possessed no record of what he had said. " As no man is obliged
to accuse himself, he would not run the risk of prevaricating."
Blunt was right; but their lordships were so annoyed at being
outwitted that they debated what to do next in high temper.
The Duke of Wharton (who had lost a great deal of money in
South Sea stock) lashed out wildly at Lord Stanhope, simply
because he was a member of the Government. Stanhope was not
feeling well. He had dined the night before with the Duke of
Newcastle and Craggs the younger—and apparently had consumed too great a quantity of champagne, burgundy and Tokay
wines. Wharton accused Stanhope of having fostered the breach
between the King and the Prince of Wales and declared that
" the government of the best princes was oftentimes made
intolerable to their subjects by ' ill ' ministers."

The insinuation that Stanhope was suffering from the great scourge of the day—venereal disease—was a deadly insult. The Earl rose in an apoplexy of rage. " My lord Stanhope spoke with so great vehemence, that finding himself taken suddenly with a violent headache, he went home and was cupped, which eased him a little. The next morning, he was let blood; and continued pretty well till about six o'clock in the evening, when falling into a drowsiness, his physicians thought fit to order him a glyster; but as he was turning himself to receive it, he fell on his face, and was instantly suffocated. The news of his death being brought to the king, his majesty was so sensibly touched with it, that he could not eat his supper, and his majesty retired for two hours in his closet, to lament the loss of so able and so faithful a minister, of whose service his majesty had so great need, at this critical juncture."[1]

As foreign secretary, Stanhope's collapse excited lively interest in all the capitals of Europe. The story of the drinking party gained wide currency. We find Madame seizing on it to provide her half-sister with a hideous piece of exaggerated gossip. " Lord Stanhope died as the result of a horrible orgy he had with four other lords. They have all been at death's door, and two recovered, one because blood burst out of his ears, and the other because a blood vessel burst while he was asleep. I don't understand what pleasure people find in excesses which are really only suitable for beasts . . ."[2]

Stanhope's demise was counter-balanced by a second ministerial death a week later. No one could pretend that the loss of the younger Mr. Craggs was a blow to the Government. He was heavily implicated in arranging the bribes that the South Sea Company had given. He died of small-pox, which he caught at the house of Lady March. Luckily his death occurred a few days before the Committee's first report was published. The Government was able to turn it to account by burying him in Westminster Abbey with full honours. The Speaker of the House

[1] *The Political State of Great Britain.*   [2] *Letters of Madame:* Ed. Scott Stevenson.

served as one of the pall-bearers, and Mr. Pope wrote an astonishing inscription for the tomb:

Statesman, yet Friend to Truth! of soul sincere
In Action faithful, and in Honour clear,
Who broke no promise, serv'd no private end,
Who gained no title, and who lost no friend . . .

The cases of four members of the Government were scheduled to be heard: Charles Stanhope, John Aislabie, the Earl of Sunderland and the elder Craggs. Mr. Stanhope was the first to stand trial—if it can be called a trial. The parts of the report mentioning his activities were read out, a debate followed, and a vote was taken. Stanhope was accused of having accepted a bribe of £10,000; also of having bought £50,000 of South Sea stock which was, in fact, worth £250,000, and of pocketing the difference. Stanhope was fortunate in having a father who was heir to the Earl of Chesterfield. The family rallied round, lobbied members of both Houses, distributed bribes (so it was said) and persuaded the minister's brokers to say that they had purchased the £50,000 of shares without his knowledge. As for the £10,000, Stanhope claimed that he had paid Knight in full for the stock. "You have heard of Mr. Stanhope's acquittal by a majority of three," wrote Mr. Brodrick, Chairman of the Committee of Secrecy, "which has put the town in a flame, to such a degree as you cannot easily imagine: what consequence it may have I cannot imagine; these I think will be more or less by what shall be done to-morrow, when Mr. Aislabie's case comes on. Lord Stanhope[1] (son to Lord Chesterfield) carried off a pretty many, by mentioning in the strongest terms the memory of the late lord of that name: between forty and fifty who could not bring themselves to give negatives, were however persuaded to withdraw before the question. On the other hand, a great many of the affirmatives are gone out of town in the utmost rage, many of them not really displeased at what had happened, since

[1] Not to be confused with Earl Stanhope.

it affords but too good a handle for fermenting greater discontent
in the country. I own, I think it a very bad piece of policy, for
the whole kingdom are enraged against the South Sea scheme,
and not less so, against those who support their abettors."[1]

The next minister to be judged was Mr. Aislabie. He was not
so lucky, for no one raised a finger for him. His case was thought
" too bad," he had no influential connections, and was not much
liked. Brodrick noted with satisfaction that Walpole's corner
" sat as mute as fishes." The main allegations against the ex-
Chancellor were that he appeared to have made a profit of over
£1,000,000 on the South Sea scheme. He had a balance of nearly
£800,000 with his brokers, and he had run an account with one
of the directors, Mr. Hawes (formerly Aislabie's clerk as Secretary
to the Treasury), from which he was believed to have collected
£300,000. He had been told to produce the account book kept
by Mr. Hawes, but said that he had burned it. There were many
other allegations. He had received huge gifts of free stock; he
had accepted payments from friends in return for putting their
names on the subscription lists; he had allowed Treasury Bills
to be lent out by the Company as security on stock. The evidence
was mostly hearsay; there were no material witnesses and it
would not have stood up in a court of law. However, he was
found guilty by a unanimous vote, expelled from the House and
sent to the Tower. As his coach rolled through the city the
delighted population lit bonfires. At last they had a victim.

Next came Lord Sunderland. Walpole had been reserving his
strength for this moment. With Earl Stanhope dead, Sunderland
must be saved at any cost. Although he hated Sunderland, he
knew that the Government would not survive if he were found
guilty; the King would be obliged to send for the Tories, and
perhaps even the odious Bolingbroke would return. Sunderland
was accused of having received a bribe of £50,000. Walpole
conducted his defence with all the skill of an experienced barrister.
On the day of the debate he secured an adjournment to allow time

[1] *Parliamentary History.*

to call witnesses. Then he astonished the opposition by attacking the validity of the Committee's report. The Chairman, Mr. Brodrick, considered the evidence, which stemmed from Sir John Blunt, as foolproof. Walpole set out to discredit Blunt. Blunt had sworn on oath that he had heard Knight tell two witnesses that Sunderland had been given £50,000 of stock. The two witnesses were called to the bar. One said that Sir John Blunt could not have heard what was said because he was not in the room when Knight had spoken to them; the other said that Blunt was in the room but out of hearing distance. Although there were three humbler witnesses who claimed to have heard the same sort of conversation, Walpole succeeded in raising so much doubt as to Blunt's veracity, that when the vote was taken at eight in the evening, Sunderland was acquitted by 233 votes to 177.

The last minister scheduled to be heard was the elder Craggs. He was deeply involved in the scandal and gossip predicted that he would be found guilty by a large majority. However, he cheated his judges by taking an over-dose of opium the night before he was to appear. He had been in a deep state of melancholia ever since the death of his beloved son, and could not face disgrace with the purpose of his life extinguished. By virtue of this act (which could have been an accident but was not regarded as such), the House found him guilty and ordered his estates to be confiscated.

Now it was time to punish the directors. The House had voted to apply their estates " to the relief of the unhappy sufferers of the South Sea Company." What portion, if any, should the owners be allowed to retain? Mr. Brodrick's brother, St. John, was in favour of the most extreme penalties. " After all the pains that have been taken to detect the villainies of the directors and their friends, I am afraid they will at last slip through their fingers, and that nothing further will be done as to confiscation, hanging, etc. There certainly is a majority in the House of

Commons that are willing to do themselves and the kingdom justice; but they act so little in concert together, that they are constantly baffled by a set of men whom guilt, money, etc. have linked in closest bond . . . The House were five hours in a committee last Friday upon the director's bill, and were amused and bantered the whole time by questions and amendments proposed by Skreen, etc. so that they rose at last without coming to any resolution."[1]

The directors were not hanged, but the House was far from lenient. It went into Grand Committee and debated the case of each director in turn. Sir John Fellows was the first on the list. His estate amounted to £243,096. A gentleman named Mr. Sloper moved that since " it did not appear that he had been so active in the late vile and pernicious practices as some others, owing perhaps rather to the heaviness than the purity of his mind, that he might be allowed £20,000." But the House considered this too generous and reduced it to £10,000. Next came Sir Charles Joye. He had played an active part in the " nefarious dealings" and was allowed only £5,000 out of £40,105. The director who came off best was Sir Theodore Janssen with £50,000 out of £243,244; when he put up his estate, Wimbledon Manor, for sale, the Duchess of Marlborough bought it. The director who fared worst was Mr. Francis Hawes, the Receiver-General of Customs. The House would not forgive him for his secret dealings with Mr. Aislabie, and worse, his failure to produce his account book, saying that Aislabie had burned it. He was allowed £31 out of £40,031.

The most interesting debate centred on Sir John Blunt. *The Parliamentary History* describes it as follows:

" Mr. Laurence Carter moved to allow him only 1s.; Lord James Cavendish £1,000 and Mr. Plummer £5,000; Sir Joseph Jekyll moved for £10,000; and was seconded by General Ross, Lord Molesworth, Mr. Jefferies and Mr. Windsor, who all spoke very warmly on his behalf; alleging, that he had been more

[1] *Parliamentary History.*

ingenuous in his examination before the Secret Committee, than any of the late directors; and had let them into a great many secrets, which otherwise they could not have known. To this it was answered, by Mr. Sloper, Mr. Milner, Mr. John Smith and Mr. Horatio Walpole, ' That he had been the chief contriver and promoter of all the mischief, and therefore ought to be most severely punished.'

" Mr. Sloper added, That he was grown to that height of pride and insolence last summer, that he could not give a civil answer to persons far above him. And thereupon instanced in his behaviour one day, at the treasury, of which he was himself witness, when a relation of a great man, asking Sir John for a subscription, the upstart knight, with a great deal of contempt, bid him go to his cousin Walpole, and desire him to sell his stock in the Bank, and by that means he might be supplied. Hereupon

" Mr. Robert Walpole shewed, That Sir John Blunt was a projector of many years' standing; and had been the author of several fallacious schemes, by which unwary people had been drawn in to their utter ruin. And to this purpose, instanced a project for a linen manufactory; but

" Mr. Horatio Walpole said thereupon, That was not his first; for there was a gentleman that sat next to him (meaning Mr. Jessop), whom Sir John had drawn into a project for bringing Water to London from a great distance, which was to out-do the New River Water, by which the subscribers lost all their money, though Sir John himself got some thousands by it.

" This was confirmed by Mr. Jessop himself; nevertheless the

" Lord Hinchingbroke moved for allowing Sir John Blunt £10,000 urging, That the Secret Committee had promised him favour for his openness in his examination; upon which

" General Ross desired, That the noble member who spoke last might explain himself, since he seemed to intimate, as if the Secret Committee had used underhand dealings. Adding, that for his part he knew of no promise ever made to Sir John Blunt upon that account; that he was sure he never made any; and he believed he could answer for all the rest, that there never was any such thing intimated to Sir John.

"The Lord Hinchingbroke replied, that if that honourable member would repeat his words as he spoke them, he would explain himself:

"Upon which the matter dropped. Then the question being put, for allowing Sir John Blunt £1,000 it was carried in the affirmative, by 138 votes against 94."

The final list was as follows:[1]

Persons	Estates	Allowance
Sir John Fellows, sub-Governor	£243,096	£10,000
Charles Joye, Esq., deputy Governor	£40,105	£5,000
Mr. Astel	£27,750	£5,000
Sir John Blunt	£185,349	£1,000
Sir Lam. Blackwell	£83,529	£10,000
Sir Robert Chaplin	£45,875	£10,000
Sir Wm. Chapman	£39,161	£10,000
Mr. Chester	£140,372	£10,000
Mr. Child	£52,437	£10,000
Mr. De la Porte	£17,151	£10,000
Mr. Eyles	£34,329	£20,000
Mr. Edmondson	£5,365	£3,000
Mr. Gibbon	£106,543	£10,000
Mr. Gore	£38,936	£20,000
Mr. Hawes	£40,031	£31
Sir W. Hammond	£22,707	£10,000
Mr. Horsey	£19,962	£10,000
Mr. Holditch	£39,527	£5,000
Sir Theo. Janssen	£243,244	£50,000
Sir Jacob Jacobson	£11,481	£11,000
Mr. Ingram	£16,795	£12,000
Sir John Lambert	£72,508	£5,000
Sir Harcourt Master	£11,814	£5,000
Mr. Morley	£1,869	£1,800
Mr. Page	£34,817	£10,000

[1] *Parliamentary History.* If Knight's estate is added to the list the total sum confiscated amounts to about £2,000,000.

Col. Raymond	£64,373	£30,000
Mr. Read	£117,297	£10,000
Mr. Reynolds	£18,368	£14,000
Mr. Sawbridge	£77,254	£5,000
Mr. Tillard	£19,175	£15,000
Mr. Turner	£881	£800
Mr. Surman, deputy-cashier	£131,321	£5,000
Mr. John Grigsby, accomptant	£31,687	£2,000

All the directors appealed against the verdict, but only four decisions were revised. The allowance to Sir Lambert Blackwell was raised from ten to fifteen thousand pounds, mainly because he had so many friends in the House, and that to Mr. Astel from five to ten thousand pounds because his wife and child had been burned to death in a fire and he proved that he had been so distraught he had taken no part in the South Sea board meetings. The allowance to Mr. Hawes and Sir John Blunt were both raised to five thousand pounds, in the first case because £31 was considered too invidious, and in the second because the Secret Committee had promised Sir John special consideration. Mr. Pope could not resist taking a jibe at Sir John's sanctimonious strictures against party politics and his plea for brotherly love.

'Twas no court-badge, great Scrivener! fir'd thy brain
Nor lordly luxury, nor city gain:
No, 'twas thy righteous end, asham'd to see
Senates degen'rate, patriots disagree,
And nobly wishing, party-rage to cease,
To buy both sides and give thy country peace.

VII

THE END OF THE AFFAIR

NEVER had the Duchess of Kendal or Madame Kielmansegge been a target for so much abuse. Although these ladies had been named in the report laid before the House of Commons as having received £10,000 bribes, they had not been referred to since. Ministers and directors had been punished but " The Maypole " and " The Elephant " went their way undisturbed. The public was particularly enraged by the Duchess whom it regarded as a South Sea ringleader. Not only had she used her influence to get the original Bill passed, but she had helped Knight to escape as well. Even more unforgivable, she had sold out her stock in June, netting a profit of £70,000. " We have been ruined by . . . whores," wrote the *Weekly Journal* of May 28th, " nay, what is more vexatious, old ugly whores! such as could not find entertainment in the most hospitable hundreds of the old Drury."

This unpleasant observation was buried in the middle of a long, dull pro-Jacobite article, but soon it was quoted in every tavern in London. The owner of the newspaper, Mr. Mist, was summoned to the Bar of the House and accused of seditious libel— not for his attack on the ladies, but his praise of the Stuarts. He was found guilty and packed off to Newgate.

The King's popularity was not enhanced by the hatred for his mistresses. When he addressed the Lord Mayor and Aldermen of the City of London, his ministers advised him to add, " I am truly concerned at the calamity brought upon you by the wicked management of affairs in the South Sea Company; I have however this comfort, that the reproach of any part of this misfortune cannot with the least Justice be imparted to me." Not that George himself cared much what the public thought. He had no wish to govern Britain and was only happy when he could escape to the tranquil atmosphere of Hanover. Nevertheless, so long as the monarch held the power of appointment, he was the true ruler. The great world was compelled to curry his favour and intrigue for his approval. He demonstrated his power in his support for Lord Sunderland. The Earl had been acquitted by the House of Commons, but the Whig Party did not feel that his majority was large enough for him to continue as First Lord of the Treasury. He resigned his office, and Walpole took his place, becoming Chancellor of the Exchequer as well. On this showing, Sir Robert should have been chief minister, but the King would not hear of it. Sunderland was the only Englishman he really liked. He made him Groom of the Stole, which carried cabinet rank, and continued to shower him with favours. This settled the matter. Sunderland remained first minister and Walpole did the work.

Sir Robert's first task was to clear up the South Sea mess. His engraftment scheme had been stillborn, since neither the Bank nor the East India Company wished to take over South Sea stock. So now he had to begin all over again. Things were easier, for the worst of the panic was over, and the finances had begun to cure themselves. His job mainly was to inject order. The blow to the national credit had been largely psychological. Many people had lost, but an equal number had gained. The money was still there, but in strange pockets. Other money, which had not been risked, was tucked away in bags of gold. Only confidence could start it circulating again.

Walpole set about to restore that confidence by simple methods. He pointed out that trade was good, and, with no wars threatening, prospects for the future unusually bright. Once again he emphasised that there could be no repudiation of South Sea contracts. With this prerequisite clearly understood, he presented a brief redistribution scheme. The Company possessed surplus stock amounting to £8,000,000, apart from the £2,000,000 it had mulcted from the directors. This would be distributed to shareholders on a basis of £33 for every hundred pounds of capital stock held. A further small distribution would be made to annuity holders who had converted in August. All stock, whether bought in May or August was fixed, for purposes of reckoning, at 400. People who had borrowed money from the Company on the security of their stock could free themselves from future obligations by paying 10% and forfeiting their holdings.

These were the main points of Walpole's reorganisation plan. The public had expected the Government to bear more of their losses, and a howl of rage went up from those who had been hit the hardest. After the second reading of the Bill at the end of July, hundreds of angry investors stormed the lobbies of the House of Commons. They thrust leaflets into the hands of members saying, " Pray do justice to the annuitants, who lent their money on Parliamentary security." In the middle of the debate the Speaker was informed that the crowd was growing " riotous and tumultuous." He sent for the Justices of the Peace for the City of Westminster, and instructed them to bring constables with them. When the Justices arrived they addressed the crowds and asked them to clear the lobbies. The people angrily refused. After the Riot Act was read twice, the Justices warned the crowd that if they persisted in remaining for the third reading, they would have to suffer the consequences of the Act. Luckily, they dispersed, shaking their fists, shouting insults, and crying out arguments above the tumult. They had come as peaceful subjects, they said, to represent their grievances, and had not expected to be treated like a mob of scoundrels. " You first pick our pockets," shrilled someone, " then you send us to gaol for complaining."

Once Walpole's scheme became law, the country drifted back to normal. The dissatisfied knew there was no further hope of redress, and gradually complaints were reduced to grumbles. The South Sea Company continued its existence for many years, largely because liquidation was too complicated. For a while it

Sir Robert Walpole who rose to power after the collapse of the South
Sea Bubble

dabbled unsuccessfully in whale fishing off Greenland. Then in 1733 its capital was divided into four parts, and three quarters used to form a new concern whose sole purpose was issuing annuities. Not until 1854 was the remainder of the Company's stock paid off, and its business wound ·

Soon after the near-riots in the House of Commons, a sensation was created by the arrival in England of Mr. John Law. The last we saw of this gentleman was in the summer of 1720, when he was hiding in his house at St. Cloud for fear of the wrath of the populace. In the autumn he plucked up courage and began to wander from one house to another—always his own. He had bought twenty-six estates with his Mississippi profits, which were scattered throughout France, and were worth half a million pounds. Although the public clamoured for his blood, and there were frequent rumours that he was to be hanged, the Regent refused to sacrifice him. The Duc de Bourbon, who was sheltering Law's wife and children at Chantilly, finally secured a passport for him; in December he left France on a few hours' notice and went to Brussels. There he was hailed as a great man. The Marquis de Prie gave a banquet for him and other big-wigs entertained him at the theatre. He had left France with no money; all he had was a pension of £1,000 a year which was paid to him personally by the Regent. His creditors, however, still regarded him as a rich man and pursued him for debts amounting to more than £100,000. He had hopes that once the Mississippi finances were straightened out, he would be allowed to sell his estates and use his capital. Meanwhile, he moved from city to city, fleeing from writs that would land him in a debtors' prison. Finally he decided to go to England, and enlist support for the return of his property among powerful nobles who might have influence with the Regent.

Oddly enough, Mr. Law held himself in no way to blame for the Mississippi catastrophe. He had recovered from his fright and depression, and convinced himself that his " system " was sound;

it had only failed because of opposition, over-enthusiasm, lack of co-operation. He had endless excuses which he cited to all who would listen. He kept up a relentless correspondence with the Regent and the Duc de Bourbon, pressing his claim to his estates —which were now in the hands of the Government—and begging to be allowed back to settle his affairs. He received sympathetic answers, but was told that emotions were still high, and it would not be safe for him to return.

Soon after his arrival in England, he was received by the King, and obtained his pardon. He took a house in Conduit Street and settled down to await developments. He had luxurious tastes and found it impossible to live on his thousand a year. He wrote to the Countess of Suffolk, who was a distant relation of Lady Catherine Law, and asked if she could persuade the Duke of Argyll (one of Law's supporters) to supplement his pension. " Can you not prevail on the Duke to help me something more than the half year? Or is there nobody that could have good nature enough to lend me one thousand pounds? I beg that, if nothing of this can be done, that it may only be betwixt us two, as I take you as my great friend; and I am very well assured of it by the honour I had done me yesterday at court by the King. I had another letter yesterday from France, with the same thing over again. Excuse this, dear madam, and only put yourself in my place, and know, at the same time, that you are the only friend I have. Yours &c. Law."[1]

Two years passed and the Regent's letters grew more encouraging. He told Law that he still had faith in his financial ability and would like to have him back. This contingency did not escape the attention of Sir Robert Walpole, who, upon Lord Sunderland's death in 1722, had become first minister. In April, 1723, he wrote to the British Ambassador in Paris. " I know not what is certainly to be determined . . . in regard to Mr. Law. If the Duke of Orléans is disposed to recall him, as Mr. Law's friends here are very sanguine in hoping, it is not our business to

[1] *Life of John Law of Lauriston*: John Philip Wood.

obstruct it. But it is not easy to judge what is most to be wished for in this case, unless we know the competition, and upon whom the favour and confidence of the Duke of Orléans might probably fall. If Mr. Law does not return, there can be no doubt but that the power might fall into worse hands; and if any who are neither Englishmen by birth or affection should prevail, we should have a less chance than by admitting one who has sundry ties to wish well to his native country. But, perhaps, Mr. Law's being thought agreeable or acceptable in England would not at all forward his return to France; for nothing but his being thought not only an able but a good Frenchman can secure his being recalled."[1]

Law's bright hopes came to naught, for in December, 1723, the Regent died. (His mother, Madame, who had believed that her son would precede her to the grave, had died a year earlier.) From then on Law had few prospects. He was estranged from his wife who lived in Brussels and Utrecht; his pension had stopped with the Regent's death, and he saw little hope of salvaging his property. Although the Duc de Bourbon had made three million pounds through Law's system he offered him no financial assistance. Worse still, Bourbon was now Prime Minister of France, but would not risk unpopularity by pleading for him. In 1724 Law wrote the Duke that "there was scarcely an example, perhaps not one instance, of a stranger like him who acquired, in so high a degree, the confidence of the Prince, who made so large a fortune in so upright a manner, and who, on leaving France, reserved nothing for himself and family, not even what he had brought into the kingdom with him."[2] He enclosed a pathetic memorial in which he emphasised that he had sacrificed everything for the Mississippi Company, "even my property and my credit, being now bankrupt, not only in France, but also in other countries. For them I have sacrificed the interests of my children, whom I tenderly love, and who are deserving of all my affection; these children, courted by the most considerable

---

[1] *Life of John Law of Lauriston:* John Philip Wood.
[2] *Works:* John Law.

families in France, are now destitute of fortune and of establishments. I had it in my power to have settled my daughter in
marriage in the first houses of Italy, Germany, and England; but
I refused all offers of that nature, thinking it inconsistent with my
duty to, and my affection for, the state in whose service I had the
honour to be engaged. I do not assume to myself any merit from
this conduct, and I never so much as spoke upon the subject to the
Regent. But I cannot help observing, that this mode of behaviour
is diametrically opposite to the idea my enemies wish to impress
to me; and surely all Europe ought to have a good opinion of my
disinterestedness, and of the condition to which I am reduced
since I no longer receive any proposals of marriage for my
children."[1]

Law was not the only one who suffered. French methods were
very different from those of England. The Regent allowed his
subjects to be fleeced to the last hair on their heads. Promises
were broken, obligations dishonoured, every possible advantage
seized by the state. Thousands had been ruined by speculation,
now the Government deliberately set out to ruin thousands more.
People who had been prudent enough to profit from the Mississippi scheme were ordered to reveal the sums they had made, and
told that they would be penalised.

This was an astonishing move since the speculators had committed no crime; indeed the Government had encouraged them,
by every means in its power, to invest in the Company. The idea
was rendered even more unjust by the fact that the nobles were
exempted. The aristocracy had always been immune from
taxation, now their immunity was extended to their Mississippi
gains. The reason for this extraordinary action was rooted in the
State's deep dedication to the principle of privilege and in-
equality. The nobles refused to tolerate the fact that people of
small account had made fortunes. This decision was put into effect
by an edict of July, 1721, which announced that all persons who
had been poor two years earlier and now possessed " riches above

[1] *Life of John Law of Lauriston:* John Philip Wood.

their condition " would be heavily fined. The fines were so large they frequently took 90% of a man's possessions—particularly if the man had the lowly status of a blacksmith or a footman.

This act alone gives one a clear idea why the French Revolution was inevitable and only makes one wonder why it came no sooner. It also offers a sharp contrast between the Governments of England and France. Although we look upon the Britain of 1720 as steeped in privilege and corruption, the impartiality with which justice was meted out in England, regardless of money or position, shows how far advanced English thought was to that of the Continent. The comparative liberality of the English aristocracy explains how it managed to weather so many social changes, and even to-day continues to play a part in the life of the country.

This difference of attitude between the two nations has been reflected by historians in their judgement of the two " booms." The South Sea directors and ministers have always been branded as swindlers, whereas Mr. Law and his colleagues have come down to us as misguided but honest men. No doubt Mr. Law's intentions were honest; but the fact remains that he invested half a million pounds in land, and distributed £3,000,000 of Mississippi money in bribes to the nobility—not described as bribes but as " gifts to ensure the smooth working of the system." In England a spade was called a spade.

In the end, it was Lady Catherine's relations who helped Law. They gave him a small allowance and in 1725 he moved to Venice where he remained until his death four years later. His spirit was not broken. He supplemented his income by gambling. He offered to pay £1,000 against a shilling to anyone who could throw double sixes six times running. It is surprising that anyone accepted the offer, but apparently so many people tried their luck that in the end it was Law who made the £1,000. The great Montesquieu visited him in Venice and reported that " he was still the same man, with small means, but playing high and boldly, his mind occupied with projects, his head filled with calculations."[1]

Law was 58 when he died. He was buried in Venice and the following epitaph was put on his tombstone:

> Ci git cet Ecossois célèbre,
> Ce calculateur sans égal,
> Qui, par les règles de l'algèbre
> A mis la France à l'hôpital.

Robert Walpole became first minister in 1722. The Whigs, whom he had saved, dominated the Government for over half a century. Their rule marked an era of peace and prosperity. What happened to the South Sea directors? Most of them repaired their broken fortunes by energy and hard work. They had far reaching connections in the merchant world; for example, Sir Theodore Janssen had business relations in Paris, Geneva, Amsterdam, Genoa, Leghorn, Antwerp and Dublin. Trade was flourishing, and many of them were pressed into the services of other companies. Edward Gibbon, the historian wrote that his grandfather, who had been allowed only £10,000 out of an estate of £106,000, began all over again at the age of fifty-five. " On these ruins," wrote the historian, " with the skill and credit, of which Parliament had not been able to despoil him, my grandfather at a mature age erected the edifice of a new fortune: the labours of sixteen years were amply rewarded; and I have reason to believe that the second structure was not much inferior to the first. He had realised a very considerable property in Sussex, Hampshire, Buckinghamshire, and the New River Company; and had acquired a spacious house, with garden, at Putney, in Surrey, where he resided in decent hospitality. He died in December 1736, at the age of seventy."[2]

One of the few directors who went into retirement was Sir

---

[1] *France under the Regency*: James Breck Perkins.
[2] *Memoirs*: Edward Gibbon.

John Blunt. He moved to Bath, and lived on a substantial allowance provided by his son, who had become rich in the boom. The last heard of Sir John was in 1732 when he was summoned before a Court of Chivalry and fined for having adopted the crest of the ancient family, Blount of Sodington. He refused to accept the decision and lodged an appeal. Death overtook him in January, 1733, before his case was heard.

The ministers had fared better than the directors. The heirs of James Craggs the elder were allowed to inherit the possessions he had acquired before December 1st, 1719, while Mr. Aislabie could retain the money and property in his hands before October, 1718. Consequently, the ex-Chancellor lived in comfort at his magnificent house, Studley Royal.[1] At the eleventh hour Robert Walpole had succeeded in exempting this estate (and Mrs. Aislabie's jewels) from forfeiture. Before final judgement was passed on Aislabie he was allowed to address the Lords in his defence. He did not attempt to defend the sharp practices that had been employed. But he made several trenchant points. He reminded their Lordships that a huge Parliamentary majority had passed the South Sea Bill; and he pointed out that members were well aware that the directors intended to raise the price of the stock. For how else could they collect the £7,500,000 they had promised the Government? He then referred to the policy of lending money on the Company's stock, which had been condemned as a dangerous and pernicious practice. But what about the Bank of England? Had members forgotten that " the very Bank became a bubble . . . for they entertained a scheme in imitation of the South Sea of lending money on their stock." And not, he added, " by chance or necessity, or from any engagement to raise money for the public service, but from the same spirit that actuated Temple-mills or Garaway's fishery." Since their object was " to advance their own stock . . . it was founded in the same iniquity with any other bubble." His speech was

[1] Edward VII, when Prince of Wales, often attended shooting parties at Studley Royal, which was then owned by Lord de Grey.

received in silence, for he had touched on points which members had long ago buried, beyond the reach of conscience.

It was left to Mr. Pope to immortalise the " strange distemper " that had gripped the nation.

> *At length corruption, like a general flood*
> *Did deluge all, and avarice creeping on*
> *Spread like a low-born mist and hid the sun.*
> *Statesmen and patriots plied alike this stocks,*
> *Peeress and butler shared alike the box,*
> *And judges jobbed and bishops bit the town,*
> *And mighty dukes packed cards for half-a-crown—*
> *Britain was sunk in lucre's sordid charms.*[1]

[1] *Epistle to Allen, Lord Bathurst.*

INDEX